- MODERN -
ETIQUETTE

~ MODERN ~
ETIQUETTE

Barbara Gilgallon & Sue Seddon

WARD LOCK LIMITED · LONDON

© Text and illustrations Ward Lock Limited 1988

First published in Great Britain in 1988
by Ward Lock Limited, 8 Clifford Street
London W1X 1RB, an Egmont Company

All Rights Reserved. No part of this publication
may be reproduced, stored in a retrieval system,
or transmitted, in any form or by any means,
electronic, mechanical, photocopying, recording,
or otherwise, without the prior permission of the
Copyright owners.

Illustrated by Pauline O'Boyle

Text filmset in Sabon 10½pt
by MS Filmsetting Limited, Frome, Somerset
Printed and bound in Great Britain by
William Collins Sons & Co Ltd, Glasgow

British Library Cataloguing in Publication Data
Gilgallon, Barbara
   Modern etiquette.—(Family matters).
   1. Etiquette—Manuals
   I. Title   II. Seddon Sue   III. Series
   395

   ISBN 0-7063-6641-7

CONTENTS

INTRODUCTION

The gentle mind by gentle deeds is known:
For man by nothing is so well bewray'd,
As by his manners.

Edmund Spenser (1552?–1599)

Although the days of rigid etiquette have passed, Spenser's words are still true; men and women are judged by their behaviour. Modern etiquette has its conventions but there are very few hard and fast rules. The basis of all good manners is consideration for others and an understanding of how they would like to be treated.

Unfortunately it seems that life is increasingly lived according to the gospel of go-getting, which means putting others well down the list of life's priorities. This is a short-sighted attitude as good manners are based on common sense and are designed to oil the wheels of society, making life easier and more comfortable for everyone. Ignore them and you may be seen to lack common sense, kindness and knowledge.

Needless to say, everyone, including the most thoughtful, occasionally make gaffes. Those who are the most confident carry off such embarrassing situations with panache, using their wit and good humour to navigate between the bricks they've dropped. In *Modern Etiquette* we have looked at today's possible bricks and shown how to avoid dropping them.

NB. We have not always used both masculine and feminine words in appropriate contexts, this is for reasons of brevity, not sexism.

Barbara Gilgallon and Sue Seddon 1988

EATING, DRINKING
& TABLE MANNERS

AT HOME

... a good dinner and feasting reconciles everybody.
Samuel Pepys

Sharing a meal with friends is one of the great pleasures of life. It is, however, best to be organized, whether it's an informal supper with close friends who won't mind if the cutlery doesn't match, or a more formal occasion when you're out to impress. Guest and host can relax more if things go smoothly and each knows what is expected of them.

Invitations

Unless it's a very formal occasion most invitations to dinner are made by telephone. Close friends can be asked at short notice but it's best to ask people some ten days in advance, or three weeks if you want to be certain of their company. If your friends are absent-minded, remind them by 'phone or postcard near the date. Make the invitation clear – date, time and the sort of evening it will be, so that your guests will arrive at the right time wearing suitable clothes and with some idea of who the other guests will be. Make the invitation definite; don't expect people to turn up if you've just mentioned it in passing.

How many?

How many guests you ask depends on you, the occasion, the size of your table and your budget. It has been the custom to invite even numbers so that everyone has someone to talk to at the table but odd numbers or more men than women and vice versa simply don't matter. The important thing is to invite friends because you want them to be there – don't worry if the numbers or the sexes are not even.

What time?
Dinner usually begins between eight and nine o'clock. You can eat later but if it's a weekday or friends have to get back for a babysitter, guests may have to leave before midnight. The invitation can be 8 pm for 8.30 pm, which means that you'd like people to arrive from 8 pm onwards and dinner will begin at 8.30 pm. You can also invite people for a specific time, in which case you should serve dinner half-an-hour later and guests should arrive within twenty minutes of the given time.

Arrivals
Guests should not arrive early. Anyone who has ever entertained knows that five minutes before guests are due to arrive, hosts are often scrambling into their clothes, running to the off-licence for forgotten tonics or scooping a culinary disaster from the kitchen floor. It's perfectly all right to arrive ten minutes before dinner is served – no later or you'll endanger the food.

Late arrivals
If you know you're going to be late, ring up, apologize and say when you hope to arrive. The host then knows whether to wait for you or to carry on with dinner so that the food isn't ruined. If guests are very late or don't give warning, the host should go ahead and serve dinner so that the food is at its best and the other guests don't get too hungry or drunk.

China
If you live in a stately home your table will be large enough to carry an elaborate dinner service. If you don't, then only the essentials will fit on to the average table – dinner plates, side (butter) plates, soup (if you're serving it) plates or small plates for the first course, a large serving dish for the main course and vegetable dishes.

Cutlery
Depending on the menu, you will need appropriate

cutlery for the first course, a knife and fork for the main course, a spoon and fork for the pudding and a knife for butter/cheese. Fish knives and forks and soup spoons are a help but if you don't have them, a bit of unobtrusive washing up between courses will cover the gaps. Serving spoons are essential, as is a sharp carving knife. A blunt knife is difficult to use and will make the meat you are carving look tough.

Glass
Wine buffs cringe if there isn't a separate glass for each wine served. If you entertain by the book, you will have to provide (and find space on the table for) glasses for sherry, white wine, red wine, champagne, water, liqueurs, brandy and port. Today, most people serve only one wine and guests often prefer to stick either to red or to white wine so that only one glass is needed. If you are serving water, or port and liqueurs, the glasses can be brought to the table when needed.

Place settings
There are two basic rules to remember: 1, forks on the left, knives and spoons on the right; 2, start to eat with the outside cutlery and work inwards. Butter (side)

plates are set on the left, glasses on the right, use them from right to left. Napkins, paper or linen, are folded and either put in the centre of the place setting or on the side plate. If you are pushed for space it's perfectly correct to put the pudding spoon and fork at the top of the setting. Knife blades point inwards, tines (prongs) of forks upwards.

Seating
The etiquette of seating dinner guests used to be very rigid, with a strict hierarchy. Tradition still lingers in the custom of seating the sexes alternately, but even this is disappearing now that the numbers of men and women around a dinner table may not be equal. It is easier for everyone if hosts suggest where people sit since they know their guests' interests. Making a seating plan beforehand can be useful. If the dining table is round, it is easy for everyone to join in the conversation, but rectangular tables can restrict conversation to guests sitting next to each other.

Serving
Unless you belong to the almost obsolete breed who have staff, the host has to serve everything. If you are a couple, one of you can serve food while the other makes sure that

the glasses are full. If you are solo, it's worth enlisting the help of a close friend who can pour drinks while you get things out of the oven, or alternatively ask people to help themselves. Hosts often complain that they miss out on conversation while they are busy in the kitchen. If things are going that well, take it as a compliment that your guests are deep in conversation and enjoy the sound of their chatter while you sort out the next course, joining in when you are able.

If you are organized, you won't have to leave the table for long or keep leaping up to fetch things. The first course can be put out before people come to the table, the main course can be served onto plates and passed round or the host can carry the dish to each guest serving from the left so that guests can help themselves. Everything else can be passed from guest to guest.

Order of courses

The complete order of courses shown below is very rarely served in its entirety. Three or four simple courses are the norm.

Soup or other first course; Fish; Sorbet; Meat and vegetables; Salad; Pudding; Savoury; Cheese; Fruit. Fish, sorbet and savoury are rare as individual courses. Fish is often served as the main course, salad can be served with the main course and cheese is sometimes served before pudding. Most menus today consist of a first course, main course, pudding and cheese. It's quite acceptable to serve three courses: either first course, main course and pudding; or main course, pudding, and cheese and fruit; or first course, main course and cheese.

Clearing the table

Scraping the scraps and stacking the plates at the table is off-putting, noisy and disruptive. Clear them two or three at a time stacking them on a side table or near the sink. The table is cleared of the first and second course before pudding or fruit and cheese is served.

Port, coffee and liqueurs
Port is served with cheese. The host serves the person to his/her right and then him/herself and then passes it to the left. It should be passed clockwise with guests helping themselves. Make sure that it circulates steadily. Coffee can be served at table. If you serve it in another room, remember that while it may be more comfortable it will interrupt the flow of the evening. Liqueurs are served with coffee.

Over-helpful guests
Kind offers of help will be gratefully received by solo hosts but the pouring of drinks, clearing the table and carrying in dishes is about as far as it should go. Don't leap up at the end of the main course and start the washing up as it disrupts everyone, kills the party spirit and makes other guests feel uncomfortably guilty. Most hosts want to make it an evening off for friends. If you want to help and know that the host will wash up that evening, stay and do it when everyone else has gone.

TABLE MANNERS

Modern table manners have been refined from elaborate rituals of the past. All are designed for their practicality, not for their snob value. They prevent you from digging your elbows into your neighbour, shooting food onto the floor, or spilling things into your lap. Once mastered they are unobtrusive basic skills learned to make life easy for you and everyone else.

How to hold your knife and fork
The illustration opposite shows the correct and most practical way to hold your knife and fork.

Some foods, such as peas, are almost impossible to eat without turning your fork over. That's fine, keep your elbows tucked into your side by holding your knife and fork as vertical as possible and push the peas onto the fork with the knife. Don't wield cutlery horizontally and

shovel food onto your fork as if you were clearing a building site – your elbows will do irreparable damage to your neighbour. Forks alone are used for food such as lasagne.

Show that you have finished eating by placing your knife and fork together on the plate, tines of the fork pointing upwards.

How to eat tricky foods

Artichokes Served hot with butter or cold with vinaigrette. Using your fingers, tear off each leaf, dip the broad end in the sauce and gently pull it between your teeth scraping off the flesh. Discard the leaf at the side of the plate. Scrape off the remaining fronds or choke and eat the heart with a knife and fork.

Asparagus Serve hot or cold with a sauce. Using your fingers, pick up the stalk by the end, dip the tip in the sauce and eat. Repeat the process down the stalk. If the end becomes tough discard on the side of the plate.

Corn on the cob Hold the whole cob at each end, or by the small prongs provided. Bite the corn from the cob. It's very messy and not for those without teeth.

Fish Cut the whole fish along its lateral line – an obvious line on the side of the fish. Ease the flesh off the bone and eat. Take out the backbone and discard on the side of the plate or on a plate provided for bones. Eat the other half of the fish. Bones in the mouth should be removed with the fingers with as little fuss as possible.

Fruit At extremely formal dinners fruit is peeled, quartered and eaten with a knife and fork, but this is rather stuffy. Quarter and core fruit; peel or leave the skin on if you prefer. Eat with your fingers. Slice the top off oranges, cut the skin into quarters and peel off. Break fruit into segments and eat. Grapes, cherries, etc. are eaten whole, putting your hand to your mouth with which you put the pips or stones onto the side of your plate.

Pasta This is guaranteed to spray your shirt front with sauce unless you know what you are doing. Lift a small forkful of pasta, with the tips of the tines against the edge of the plate (not against a spoon), revolve the fork and wind up the ends of the pasta.

Rolls Break in small pieces and butter piece by piece; do not cut in half and butter in one go. Bread and rolls go on the plate to your left.

Soup Put the spoon into the soup bowl at the side nearest to you, push it across sideways and lift out on the furthest edge. Drink your soup from the side of the spoon. Always tip the soup bowl away from you. When finished, rest your spoon in a large bowl or in a saucer if it is a small bowl.

Shellfish Prawns and shrimps are usually ready peeled but if not, take off the head, then the legs. The main shell will then come off easily. It's all done with the fingers so a finger bowl may be provided. Rinse the tips of your fingers in it, one hand at a time and dry on the napkin.

Mussels are usually served in shells. Either pick up by the shell and take out the mussel with a fork or use an empty shell as a scoop or pincer to get the mussel out of the shell. Do not open closed shells, discard them.

Oysters are served in half a shell. Take the flesh out with a fork and eat it then drink the juice from the empty shell.

A few do's and don'ts

Do begin to eat as soon as you are ready. If that seems churlish wait for the person next to you and begin together. If all guests wait until the host is served the food will be cold and their efforts wasted. If the host encourages you to begin eating, do so, otherwise there's a constant mantra of 'Do begin, do begin' which is boring for host and guests.

Do compliment the host on the food. It's archaic to keep quiet about it.

Don't speak with your mouth full – no-one wants to see your half-masticated food, however riveting your contribution to the conversation.

Don't put your elbows on the table – at least not until after-dinner conversation keeps you at the table.

Don't wave your knife and fork in the air while you're talking.

Don't stretch across your neighbour, ask them to pass the salt to *you*.

Don't pick up chicken bones etc. and eat them with your fingers unless the host leads the way.

Don't smoke between courses unless your host does. If it's a non-smoking household ask if you may; or better still, don't smoke at all.

To drink or not to drink

Never press anyone to drink alcohol, and never feel obliged to drink it. Non-alcoholic alternatives should always be available. Refuse more to drink by saying 'no thank you' and putting your hand across your glass to show that you mean it. Don't gulp wine, sip it. Don't rush to finish a glass if another wine is served to accompany the next course; you can either leave it or refuse the next wine.

What to do if you can't eat the food

You may, because of religious, ethical or medical reasons, not be able to eat the food that is served. If there is no choice the easiest solution is to accept a little of it and play with it a bit before putting down your knife and fork. If it is a main course accompanied by vegetables, eat the latter. If the host shows concern, you may have to explain why you can't eat everything. Explain briefly, do not go into detail and then change the subject. A good host shouldn't really comment, or should have asked, when issuing the invitation, if there is any food the guest prefers not to eat. When invited to dinner it is helpful if the guest tells the host of any taboo foods.

What to do if you choke

If you choke, put a napkin or clean handkerchief to your mouth immediately and turn away from the table if possible. If it is a really bad choking fit leave the room and recover without embarrassing yourself and fellow guests. If someone next to you chokes don't make it worse by exclaiming loudly or slapping them on the back. Make sure that they have a glass of water near them and monitor their progress discreetly without staring in horrified fascination.

What to do if you sneeze, cough, or need to blow your nose.

Should you sneeze, cough or need to blow your nose, find a clean handkerchief immediately, bury your nose and face in it, turning well away from the table. Coughing and sneezing may be unavoidable, but blowing your nose often is.

What to do if you spill or break something

Should you spill or break something, clear it up with the host's help, apologizing as you do so. Be sincere, don't go on and on with the apologies, but get back to enjoying the evening. If there are servants, they will see to everything and you shouldn't try to help. As you say goodbye, apologize again and offer to arrange and pay for any necessary cleaning. If the host is adamant in refusing but you still feel bad about the incident, you could make recompense with a gift. If you break the best crystal, etc., note the design and make, and buy a replacement. Whatever you do, don't press money into the host's hand as you leave, or offer to replace the object and then do nothing.

What to do if you need to leave the table
In formal settings try to avoid leaving the table, but if you need to go to the lavatory, leave and return with as little fuss as possible. If you feel ill you may have to tell someone, but again, do it as unobtrusively as possible. That said, don't sit through a meal in wretched anguish; other guests will be far too polite to comment if you leave, and should act as if you have been at the table all the time.

Goodbyes and thankyous
Don't linger on until the small hours of the morning if your host is becoming monosyllabic with tiredness. On the other hand, it is not polite to leave as soon as you've put your coffee cup down. If the occasion is informal and invitations were by telephone, then call the next day to say thankyou. A more formal dinner requires a written thankyou.

IN RESTAURANTS

Who pays?
There is a lot of difference between 'Let's go out for a meal' and 'I'd like to take you out to lunch/dinner'. The former means that you will share the bill, the latter that the person who issues the invitation will be treating you. It's unfair to suggest going out for a meal and then

insisting on paying. Your companions may be quite happy to share the bill, but not so happy at the thought of returning your hospitality and footing the entire bill, particularly if the restaurant is expensive.

If you are the host

Booking Always book in advance if you have invited guests out to dinner or lunch.

What to wear Tell your guest a bit about the restaurant so that they have some idea of whether to wear jeans or a little black number.

Arriving If you are arriving separately, the host should always arrive a little early, ahead of the guests. If you all arrive together the host should lead the way in and speak to the waiter about the reservation.

Ordering You can order the food (à la carte offers a choice of dishes, table d'hôte is a set menu), although the waiter will often ask each person individually. Starters and main courses are ordered at the beginning of a meal, puddings will be offered after the main course is cleared.

Wine Order the wine after checking whether the guests prefer red or white. When the waiter brings it a little is poured in to the host's glass for him/her to taste and to check the temperature, etc. If it meets with the host's approval the waiter will pour wine for everyone. The house wine is not usually poured for tasting. The waiter may leave the bottle for the host to refill the glasses, or he may return and fill the glasses at intervals.

Calling the waiter

Call the waiter by saying 'excuse me' or 'waiter' when he is in earshot. You can also raise a hand or catch his eye. Calling across the room or snapping your fingers is guaranteed to make the waiter head off in the opposite direction.

How to complain

If the food is not what you ordered, isn't properly cooked, or is not up to standard in some way, you should complain. Call over the waiter, explain courteously what is wrong and go back to your conversation, giving him no opportunity to enter into a discussion about it. There is no need to deliver a lecture or to be rude or hostile. A good waiter in a good restaurant will calmly remove it and bring back another dish. Always ask your guests if their food is all right.

The bill
Check the bill when it arrives. If it is correct, pay it together with a 10 to 15 per cent tip if service is not included. If you have to query it, do so as unobtrusively as possible; you can always go to the desk to avoid embarrassing your guests.

The guest
As a guest, when choosing food don't order the most or the least expensive food but go for a dish in the middle price range of the menu.

In pubs and wine bars
In a group at a pub or wine bar it is customary for each person in the group to buy a round. If you are drinking in a large group this can be difficult because the cost of a round can be astronomical and because not everyone will get the opportunity to buy a round before the group breaks up. The best solution is to share rounds. If someone new joins the group the person who last bought a round should offer to buy a drink.

Some older men still find it very difficult to accept a drink from a woman. In a group situation, a woman can sometimes overcome this by asking a younger man to order the drinks and give him the money for the round. If the group is small it may be better to allow an older man to do the buying rather than make him feel extremely uncomfortable. You may think that it's about time he joined the twentieth century, and that he shows a lack of consideration for women, but it is just as inconsiderate to insist on embarrassing him.

ENTERTAINING –
PARTIES & SOCIALIZING

Entertainment is the end for which, in the most part, we live.

Samuel Pepys

LET'S HAVE A PARTY

Choose the type of party to suit the occasion and the guests. Even if your granny is a game old bird, other people of advanced years prefer lunch or drinks parties, while most young friends like a party with dancing.

Lunch parties

Lunch parties have fallen out of favour because most people are at work, but Sunday lunch is very popular. Don't ask guests to arrive too early on a Sunday as they may have been up late the night before; 1 pm is early enough and many people don't begin Sunday lunch until 2 pm or 3 pm. Offer pre-lunch drinks. A roast is the traditional fare at Sunday lunch. Even if lunch begins late, guests shouldn't stay on until the evening as most people have to prepare for the coming week.

Drinks parties

Drinks parties used to be called cocktail parties but as cocktails are rarely served now, the ubiquitous 'drinks' has taken over. They are extremely useful for entertaining people whom you have only just met and would like to know better, for introducing friends to friends, for nurturing business contacts and for renewing contact with people that you don't see very often.

Drinks parties usually start between 6 pm and 6.30 pm, although pre-lunch drinks are popular at Christmas or on Sundays. Whenever they begin they do not normally last longer than about two hours. The times should be given on the invitation.

Drinks served vary between sherry, wine, cocktails (spirits mixed with fruit juices and mixers) or champagne. It is correct to serve just one, or a combination of these drinks, say sherry followed by wine, but most people prefer to serve just one kind of drink. Non-alcoholic drinks should always be available, the most popular being fruit juices and mineral water.   You should always serve food with alcohol.

Party parties

To enjoy yourself with your friends need be the only reason for throwing a party. Parties usually begin after 9 pm and can go on until the small hours. To enjoy it as much as the guests, the host must be organized. Send out written invitations three to four weeks in advance. It's quite all right to invite guests by telephone but don't forget to invite very close friends whom you may forget in the assumption that they know all about it.

Numbers

Invite about ten more people than you can comfortably accommodate. Someone is bound to have to refuse or to drop out at the last minute. Getting the numbers right is often the key to a successful party: too many and it will be very uncomfortable for the guests, too few and the party will never really get off the ground. Adjust the numbers to the size of the rooms, start the party in one room because a small area will get the party atmosphere going, then allow it to expand into adjoining rooms as it gets under way. If you hire a hall make sure that you invite enough people to fill it. There's nothing more dejecting than too few people in a large space.

Food

The food you provide depends on you, your culinary abilities and your budget. You can serve anything from bread, cheese and pâté to elaborate salads, cold meats and salmon or hot pasta dishes. You can do the food yourself or have outside caterers to come and do everything for you. If you do it yourself, remember that hot dishes will take up lots of your time at the party; whereas salads can be put out before and people can help themselves. Caterers are obviously more expensive but they will serve all the food and leave you free to circulate and enjoy yourself. In North America, some hosts provide the drinks while friends bring along food, a sensible reversal of the custom in Britain because it spreads the greatest work load. If you don't have enough china and cutlery, borrow or hire it. Put the food in an accessible place, away from dancing and drinking area.

Drinks

Wine or beer are the usual drinks at this kind of party, but whatever you serve, make sure that you have enough. It is standard practice for guests to bring a bottle, but the host should not rely on this and should provide enough to get the party well under way. A standard bottle of wine holds about six glasses, a litre about nine. A bottle of whisky or gin about twenty, depending on how large you pour them. Many wine merchants have drink-or-return sales and will hire out glasses too. Most people arrive by car so non-alcoholic drinks must be available.

Serving drinks can be a problem. You can hire someone to do it for you so that you are free to circulate; you can leave the drinks in an accessible place and get people to help themselves (but it's surprising how reticent people can be to do this); or you can do it yourself with the help of close friends who may be happy to help out in a way that gets them circulating freely.

What to wear

What to wear depends entirely on who is giving the party and how formal it will be. The host should always give some idea of the occasion so that guests will come suitably dressed. If there is no indication, ask – it's embarrassing to turn up inappropriately dressed. If you are still in doubt, pick something smart but comfortable. If the invitation says fancy dress, try to join in because it's dispiriting for the host if no-one bothers. Before you decide to have a fancy dress party give some thought to the theme. Don't pick on something so elaborate that guests will have to go to the expense of hiring costumes.

PARTY MANNERS

Hallo
It isn't vital to arrive on time but spare a thought for the nervous host anxiously waiting for the first arrival. Try to arrive within an hour of the invitation time. The host could ask a few close friends to arrive early to get the party atmosphere going. You will, of course, have set aside a room for coats. As people arrive, direct them to it (don't take them yourself or you may not be there to open the door to the next guest) and make sure they know where to get a drink when they are ready.

Kissing and hugging
Displays of affection are best reserved for close friends and family. Many people are reticent about being hugged and kissed and guest and host should play it by ear. If people arrive with a formal hallo, they may leave after a good party with a kiss and a hug.

THE DUTIES OF A PERFECT HOST
1 To make everyone at the party feel included and relaxed and to ensure that they enjoy themselves.
2 To make introductions. It will be impossible to introduce each guest individually but a good host will have thought beforehand of guests who, for a particular reason – mutual interests for example, will be interested to meet each other. Parties are about the mating game, too, and the host should always make an effort to introduce prospective partners, as some single men and women find it difficult to march up to total strangers and

introduce themselves.

3 To spend time with everyone at the party. It's bad manners to abandon most of the guests in favour of a chosen few.

4 To make a point of including guests who may not know anyone else. That definitely doesn't mean a hurried introduction at the beginning of the evening and then leaving them to it. The host should check throughout the evening that no-one is alone or stuck in a corner.

5 Breaking up male or female gaggles. Good guests shouldn't let this happen.

6 To control the general running of the party. To see that food is served at an appropriate moment, that everyone's glass is full, that ashtrays are in plentiful supply and emptied if necessary, to be available in moments of crisis – spilt drinks etc., to keep the music flowing, to answer the door and to say goodbye.

Parties can be hard work and many hosts find that a party has passed so fast that they hardly seem to have eaten or drunk or spoken to half the guests.

THE DUTIES OF A PERFECT GUEST

1 To circulate freely. Ideally a guest should be able to introduce him/herself to other guests. It takes a lot of self-possession but every party needs a few guests who can get things going and who are uninhibited enough to make fools of themselves if necessary. It isn't very helpful to the atmosphere if a guest starts talking to old friends the moment he or she arrives and sticks with the same people all evening.

2 To keep conversation flowing. That means listening to a fellow-guest and knowing how to make small talk.

3 To be aware of other guests' wishes. They may want to move on to another group and a good guest will be aware of this and enable it. Don't absolutely insist that you fetch someone a drink if they want to go themselves. It may be their only ploy to move on.

4 Not to scan the room looking for a better pitch whilst already in conversation with someone.

5 To look after him/herself: fetch drinks, take the lead in the dancing, etc.

6 If you want to take a friend to the party you must ask the host first. Numbers may be critical, caterers already booked. Think before you ask: if it is a special or family celebration it may be inappropriate to take along a stranger but it will be difficult for the host to refuse once you have asked.

7 Gate-crashers are always unwelcome and should be asked to leave. The host may need moral support in dealing with gate-crashers.

INTRODUCTIONS AND THE ART OF CIRCULATING

Introductions are full of pitfalls. It's happened to us all, you go to introduce one friend to another and her name flies straight out of your head. If that happens carry it off as well as you can, apologize and try again or turn to the friend for help. If she is a sensitive guest she'll come to your rescue straight away.

Another danger is forgetting someone's name immediately you have been introduced. One way of avoiding this is to repeat the name as you shake hands. If you do forget say 'I'm sorry, I didn't quite catch your name.' Don't forget it a second time!

Most people today are introduced by their christian and surnames, in very informal situations by christian name alone, more formally as Mrs, Miss, Mr, etc. Use the names by which people are introduced, if surnames only are used, use them until someone asks you to use their christian name. Hosts and friends should not use pet or nicknames when making introductions, but snippets of information are helpful: 'David, I'd like you to meet Ann who's just come back from China.' David should then ask Ann about her trip to China.

Who do you introduce to whom?

The convention is that men are introduced to women: 'Charles Dover, Barbara Kent'. If two people of the same sex are introduced, then the junior is introduced to the senior: commoner to royalty, Mr to Lord, twenty year-old to grandmother. Married couples should be introduced individually, they don't become 'Mr-and-Mrs-Smith' on marriage, they are John Smith and Jane Smith.

There may be someone at the party you'd like to meet. Unless you are self-assured enough to introduce yourself, ask a mutual friend or the host to introduce you.

Conversation

Chatting to people you don't know can be very intimidating, but relaxed and enjoyable social events depend on it so no-one should duck the responsibility. Introductions can help if the host has given you a lead: 'Michael, my I introduce William Brown who lives in Clayford and knows your friend Malcolm Taylor very well.' But if you are starting from scratch, opening gambits vary from 'Angela's garden always looks so marvellous, do you have a garden?' to 'Did you see that film on television last night?' You can only hope that they have and that they pick up your lead.

Each member of the group has a responsibility to make a contribution. Never give 'yes' or 'no' answers to questions, it's extremely rude and impossible for the other person to keep up the conversation. It's also rude to dominate the conversation with a subject or person known only to one or two in the group. How can the others possibly join in? Some people are naturally good at small talk, the rest of us just have to work hard at it.

It's up to the host or another member of the group to diffuse conversations that get onto sticky ground, or dangerously near rancorous argument.

Getting stuck

It can be very difficult to move on from a group in which

you're stuck. If you are very confident you can simply say 'Excuse me' and leave or make a joke of it – 'The host has paid me to circulate so I'd better earn my keep.' But those are strictly for the very self-assured. Leaving a group is easier than leaving one other person, you can hardly leave them all by themselves. You can go to the loo and hope that they've found someone else to talk to by the time you get back, or you can fetch drinks and bring someone else into the conversation when you return. If you genuinely see someone else you want to talk to, you can suggest that you go and say hallo.

Being left alone is even more of a nightmare. You can temporarily alleviate the situation by going to the loo. If you get another drink or some food you may start up a conversation with someone at the bar or table. If all that fails, and you know no-one, seek out the host and make him or her introduce you to another group, or offer to pass round drinks or food.

If you get stuck with a prima donna, a lecher, a drunk or a bore you are quite within your rights to move on. Don't be rude, just excuse yourself and head for the nearest friend. If they persist and appear to be out to embarrass you, try to avoid a scene. Explain the situation to the host or a friend and get them to divert the offender. If you are good at withering one-liners you may have to use one – but only if the situation is extreme.

Goodbye
A good guest knows when to go home. Unless you are a very close friend, don't settle down by the fire with the last of the wine if everyone else has gone home. When you leave, find the host, thank them and make your own way to the door. If you have to leave early, don't seek out the host, leave as unobtrusively as possible otherwise everyone else will think it's time to go. Leave quietly, neighbours will not want to hear your effusive goodbyes.

Telephone the next day to say thank you and to congratulate the host on a successful party.

FAMILY CELEBRATIONS

Births, christenings, engagements and weddings are all occasions when the family might come together to celebrate. The ceremonies which accompany these events do need careful planning, however, if everything is to go smoothly. In large numbers the family group is quite formidable and some tact and diplomacy may be required. The etiquette for these occasions provides the guidelines which can relieve any anxieties about 'doing the right thing'.

GETTING ENGAGED

Formal engagements are not quite as common as they used to be. Many couples prefer a quiet announcement of their plan to be married and leave it at that. Some prefer to put their savings towards the deposit on a house rather than buy an expensive ring or host a large party. Once a couple have announced that they intend to marry, however, there are certain courtesies which are usually expected. Even if the prospective husband knows his girlfriend's family well, it is still commonplace for him to ask permission to marry her. Even though this is not a legal necessity if the bride is over the age of consent, most families appreciate knowing something of the man's career prospects and future plans. Whether this is done informally over a drink or conducted like a job interview depends on the family and the personalities involved. It is worth remembering that the father may feel as nervous about the whole procedure as his prospective son-in-law.

Once both sets of parents have been informed of the engagement the couple might arrange for them to meet, especially if they have not already done so. This meeting may be preceded by an exchange of letters expressing pleasure at the news of the intended marriage.

Close friends and relatives should be informed before any written announcement is made. This may be done in a local or a national paper. In the case of a widower or widow, contact should be made with the parents of the deceased husband or wife so that they have the news first hand.

Announcements in the press are usually paid for by the bride's parents and may read as follows:

> **Mr M. R. Jones**
> **and Miss J. Wood**
> The engagement is announced between Mark, second son of Mr and Mrs D. G. Jones of Turnstile Cottage, Sevenoaks, Kent and Judith, only daughter of Mr and Mrs R. B. Wood of 45, Butler Road, Reading.

There may be minor adjustments made to the announcement if any parent is deceased or in the case of a second marriage. When everyone has heard the news, letters and cards of congratulation may arrive. These should always be answered promptly, especially if accompanied by a gift. Engagement presents are not usually too grand.

The broken engagement
It should be remembered that a broken engagement is the concern of the couple involved. Although the rest of the family should be told as soon as possible there should be no pressure on the couple to state their reason. If either party wishes to talk about the break that is fine but the information should be offered and not sought.

Whether to return the ring or not depends on the

circumstances. In many cases the girl may keep the ring and wear it on another finger. However, if it is the girl who has decided to end the engagement she may feel more comfortable returning the ring.

If either partner finds it too difficult to tell people this could be done by a parent or a close friend. A sympathetic note might be appreciated if you know the couple well.

If the wedding invitations have been sent out the invited guests should be notified as soon as possible. Notices of cancellation are usually in the same style as the invitations. A printed card is sent with the wording as follows:

Mr & Mrs R. Clark announce
that the marriage of their
daughter, Rebecca Jane to
Mr Simon Baines will not now
take place.

Wedding presents should be returned to the donors together with a brief note.

A broken engagement, whether amicable or not should not be dwelt upon too long. Once it has occurred the family and friends should be supportive without being intrusive and allow the couple the freedom to put it behind them. References to the engagement will not be particularly welcome – especially if either of the parties is entering into a new relationship.

GETTING MARRIED

The organization of a wedding can be quite a daunting prospect. There will be times during the preparations when it is hard to remember that it is supposed to be one of the happiest of family events. Wedding etiquette is helpful in this area as many of the responsibilities can be shared.

Certain decisions should be made once a couple have decided to marry.

1 Where and when to marry. The first consideration is where the marriage will take place. Both church and civil ceremonies require some notice.

2 The reception – its whereabouts and size.

3 Attendants – bridesmaids, best man, ushers.

4 Music, flowers, bells, etc.

The first consideration is where the wedding will take place. A church wedding does not necessarily entail elaborate planning. It can be as simple as you wish it to be. If you decide on a religious service the first step is to arrange an interview with a member of the clergy of the church of your choice. At this interview you will be able to discuss the form of service together with the formalities of date, time and fees. It is a good idea to have a few alternative dates in mind as some churches get heavily booked at certain times of the year. The couple should also have some idea as to the music and form of service which they would like so that they are ready to discuss this with the minister.

A church wedding may take place by several means.

Banns of Marriage The names of the couple to be married are read out in church on three Sundays prior to the marriage in their parish of residence and in the church where they are to be married. After three readings of the Banns the couple are free to marry within three months (The Banns are read again after this time has elapsed).

Marriage by Common Licence If a marriage takes place by Common Licence the Banns do not have to be read. The couple may marry in either of their parishes – as long as they are on the electoral roll. The marriage may take place with as little as a day's notice. The marriage must take place within three months.

Marriage by Special Licence This is used in exceptional circumstances such as illness or a posting abroad. The marriage may take place in an unlicenced building at any time and without any residential qualification.

Marriage by Superintendent Registrar's Certificate Persons applying for this must have lived in a district for seven days before the marriage. A notice of the wedding is entered in the Registrar's notebook which is displayed for twenty-one days. This form is most commonly used for marriages which take place outside the Church of England.

If the ceremony is to take place at a register office, this can be arranged by certificate or licence. The wedding may take place between the hours of 8 am and 6 pm. Jewish and Quaker weddings are exceptions to this, as are marriages by special licence. Two witnesses are required although neither of these have to be known to the couple.

The reception

The reception has traditionally been the responsibility of the bride's parents. Times have changed and arrangements are often more flexible. Many girls who have left home and established a career and a good salary feel that the burden of a costly wedding should not fall entirely on their parents. It is also quite acceptable for the bride-groom's parents to offer something towards the cost of the wedding. You may need to tread carefully as some people are very sensitive about such things and see their contribution as a question of pride. However, if a couple has five daughters they may be grateful for an offer of assistance from the groom's family.

A way of getting around such a problem is to create a pool in which the engaged couple and both sets of parents contribute, or for the groom's parents to offer to pay for a specific item such as the wedding cake and the champagne. If the couple wish to extend the celebration in any way – with a party in the evening, for example – they should pay for this themselves.

A reception may be held anywhere – in a garden, at a hotel or a restaurant. The nature of the catering really depends on the time of the wedding and the available resources. Caterers will give quotes for anything from an elaborate wedding breakfast to a light buffet. If you are using outside caterers try to contact those recommended by friends and ask for several estimates from different firms.

You may, of course, decide to take on the catering yourself. It is possible to do this very successfully in families where everybody is willing to help and take on different tasks. On the other hand it can be a nightmare, just adding extra worry at a time when everything should be running smoothly. It can spoil the day if the family are worn out by the preparations.

Guests

When the size of the reception has been decided the guest list is made up. This is usually divided equally between the two families, except in cases where there are many more relations on one side than the other. The best way of working out who is to be invited is to indicate to the groom's family the maximum number of guests from their side of the family. The groom's parents then make out their own list and send it back together with names and addresses. If the guest list has to be shortened for any reason the grooms' family should be told and consulted about which names to take from the list. When the list has been finalized the invitations may be ordered and sent out about six weeks before the date of the wedding.

Attendants

It is only necessary to have ushers at large weddings. Their task is to show people to their seats in the church – the bride's family on the left and the bridegroom's on the right. The immediate family sit in the front pews.

Bridesmaids are chosen from unmarried relations and friends and they do not have to be of the same religion as the bride. If the bride wishes to ask a married sister or friend to be an attendant she is known as the matron of honour and carries out the duties of a chief bridesmaid. These are basically to shepherd the other bridesmaid along and to take the bride's flowers at the appropriate moment.

The bridegroom chooses his best man from his close friends or relations. He does not have to be a bachelor.

Who pays for what
The following is meant as a guideline. Today many of the costs of a wedding are shared. The important matter is to decide who is paying for what beforehand so that everyone has an idea of the sum they are likely to have to spend.

The clothes
Traditionally the bride's parents pay for the wedding dress although nowadays the bride often pays for it herself, if only to give herself more freedom to choose a style which she prefers. It is not unusual for the bridesmaids to pay for their own dresses. If this is the case the bride must ensure that the style of dress is one that can be adapted and used for another occasion after the wedding.

The ushers and the best man pay for any hire of clothes for themselves.

The reception, wedding cake, bride and bridesmaids' cars to the church, flowers and decorations, flowers and music at the reception, photographer and invitations are usually paid for by the bride's parents.

The fees for the ceremony, the wedding ring, presents for the bridesmaids and their flowers, buttonholes, transport for himself and the best man to the church and for his bride to the reception are paid for by the groom.

Wedding presents

The wedding present list has become the norm although it is not liked by everyone. It stems from the practical consideration that not many homes really need two toasters or five pepper mills. It is drawn up by the couple and circulated to those who ask to see it. It should include a variety of items from the least expensive to the grand. No more than two or three lists should be out at any one time as this defeats the object and leads to duplication.

It really is a good idea to ask for things which you will use and treasure for years. If, for instance, you would like a very expensive dinner service, it is a good idea to break it down into smaller groups e.g. six dinner plates, six side plates, a gravy dish etc. In this way you can build up a set without asking anyone to bear the whole expense.

The practice of putting wedding presents out on show is no longer as popular as it once was. They could be kept together in one part of the house just in case anyone asks to see them. If you do decide to display them a list should be made of anyone who sent gifts of money – without, of course, putting the amount.

The ceremony

If at all possible it is a good idea to have a rehearsal, perhaps the day before. This has the very practical use of settling everyone's nerves a little. The bride's father leads her to the altar. This duty can also be performed by an uncle or close family friend. The minister will be able to tell everyone concerned where to sit or stand. The rehearsal also has the advantage of helping the participants to work out the level at which their voice can be heard. This varies from church to church. The guests feel very cheated if they cannot hear the marriage vows being made. The bride and her father can also work out the pace at which they will move down the aisle. The slow measured walk of the bridal group needs to be practised as nerves can easily turn it into a quick gallop.

On the day, the bridegroom and best man should arrive at least twenty minutes before the bride and the bridesmaids about five minutes later. Although it has always been seen as the bride's prerogative to be late this should not become excessive. Five minutes at the most.

Reception rituals

The guests are received by the bride and groom. Both sets of parents also join the receiving group although when there are a large number of guests this may be impractical.

After the food and drink have been served speeches may be made. The traditional speeches are as follows:

1 A toast to the bride and groom is made by the bride's father or an old family friend.

2 The bridegroom makes a speech of thanks to the bride's parents for the reception and for their daughter. The guests are also thanked for their presents. The toast is 'The bridesmaids'.

3 The best man thanks the bridegroom on behalf of the bridesmaids and thanks the hosts. He may then propose a toast to the health of both sets of parents.

The best man's speech is usually the one which creates the most mirth. It can be awkward if this degenerates into a repetition of risqué remarks. If the bride and bridegroom take this in good part and the guests are the sort who would enjoy the joke, this is fine. If, however, it is likely to cause embarrassment or offence, leave it out

Finally the bride's father may thank everyone for coming and for their good wishes.

There is nothing to prevent the bride making her own speech if she so wishes. This may be to thank her parents or any individual who has helped her in preparing for the wedding.

Cutting the cake

Everyone's attention should be drawn to the fact that the

cake is to be cut. The bride makes the first cut with the help of the bridegroom. It is then removed to be sliced and distributed. The bride and groom should try and circulate and speak to all of their guests if at all possible. For their part the guests should allow the couple to move on and not monopolize them.

BIRTHS AND CHRISTENINGS

The arrival of a new baby in the family is usually a happy and joyous occasion. It can also be very exhausting. Not only do the parents have to cope with broken nights and nappies but also a stream of relatives and friends, all anxious to see the baby. Close relatives should be told of the birth as soon as possible, usually by the father. If the baby is born in the middle of the night it is better to wait until the morning – unless you know that someone has waited up for news. To spread the news more widely most parents send out cards. They might also place an announcement in a local or national newspaper, e.g.,

WELLINGS. On 1st July at St Mary's Hospital, Paddington, to Maureen and Ben a daughter, Katherine.

A single mother might announce the birth as follows:

RANDALL. On 7th February, at Queen Charlotte's Hospital, to Sarah a son, Martin.

If a name has not yet been chosen for the baby this can just be omitted.

Registering a birth

In England and Wales a birth must be registered at the office of the Registrar of Births for the district in which the birth took place within forty-two days. Some hospitals have facilities for registration on site. Both parents do not have to be present as only one signature is required. In Scotland the time limit is twenty-one days. In the case of unmarried parents the father's name may be entered on the birth certificate as long as both parents are present at the registration. Otherwise a father may make a formal declaration witnessed by a solicitor on a form available from the Registrar. The father's name may also appear on a certificate if the mother produces an affiliation form, naming him. Once the birth has been registered a short certificate, omitting details of the parents, is given free of charge. A longer certificate is supplied for a fee. The short certificate is sufficient for later requirements such as passports.

Visiting

If you wish to visit a mother and baby at home do ring to see when it is convenient to do so. If mother and baby are resting or sleeping your visit will not be very welcome. Check with hospitals as to visiting times. Good friends will make their visit brief. If there are young children in the family, draw them into the whole experience. A small gift for them as well as the baby helps them to feel that they are just as important as this newcomer. Early days can be made much smoother by friends and neighbours offering to take the other children to the park or inviting them to tea. Arriving with a casserole or a homemade pie is as welcome as a huge bunch of flowers.

The mother of a first baby is also particularly vulnerable to a torrent of well-meaning advice. By the time that she has heard several variations on a theme of bringing up wind she may be feeling less than confident. Visitors should always be tactful with their comments. The proud parents may be devastated by a thoughtless remark. New born babies are not always a picture of beauty but mistimed comments such as, 'Doesn't she look like Uncle Arthur?' can be taken the wrong way. Similarly, remarks about names, especially if they are unusual, can be quite hurtful. Most parents spend a great deal of time choosing a name for their child. If you don't like it just don't mention it. If asked you can always say, 'Its very unusual' – which is reasonably ambiguous.

The christening

This can either be a small private baptism in a church or take place during a service. Arrangements are made with the minister of the relevant church. The celebration which follows has no set form. It can be an extended family lunch, a tea party or champagne and caviar. It should be relaxed and enjoyable for all concerned.

Godparents

It is very flattering to be asked to be a godparent. The invitation implies both trust and high regard on the part of the parents. As there is usually, in the form of service, some allusion to the future safeguarding of the child's Christian commitment, it is usual for the godparents to be baptized Christians. In the Church of England a boy has two godfathers and one godmother and a girl, two godmothers and one godfather. Roman Catholics normally have one godmother and one godfather.

Godparents usually buy the baby a gift which will have some lasting value – a piece of jewelry or silver, for example. Some people like to be more practical and open a savings account in the child's name. As their godchild grows up godparents should remember birthdays and Christmas. The relationship is quite a special one and can be very useful during difficult times in later life. The sympathetic ear of someone outside the immediate family can be very helpful, particularly during adolescence.

CHILDREN

HELP WITH THE CHILDREN

There will almost certainly be times during the years when you are raising your child or children when you will need some assistance looking after them. The nature of the help you will require for your children depends on many factors. Whether you need a full time nanny or the occasional babysitter, any person with whom you leave your children should have your full trust and support. Good communication is absolutely vital if arrangements are to work well.

Nannies and mothers' helps

The level of responsibility which is placed on a person's shoulders should be in proportion to their experience and training. A fully trained nanny would expect to take charge of most of the areas which concern the children. Both the parent and the nanny should acknowledge each other's expertise – one as an expert in child care and the other as an expert on their own child. Neither the nanny or the employer should make instant judgements about each other. It can take weeks and months for the child to settle down to a new routine and allowances should be made on both sides for this.

If there is a problem it does no good to bottle it up. If there is a feeling of frankness from the beginning it helps enormously. Disputes between parents and helpers should never occur in front of the children. This can be upsetting and confusing for them – especially if they feel they are to blame. Mother's helps do not usually 'live in' but take care of the child for a fixed number of hours per day. Mothers may feel quite sensitive at the beginning. Often they will be going back to work after a break and this can produce stress. There may be worries about leaving the child as well as a desire to create a good impression at work. Life can become very difficult if the helper arrives late in the morning or cancels at short notice.

Au pairs

The situation of an au pair is rather different. They live with the family and are treated much as an older son or daughter. This means that they receive pocket money and eat with the family. In return they give some help with the children and do some light household chores. The au pair should be given time to study and to go to English classes since the primary aim of their visit is to improve their English. It is important that the workload is fair from the beginning. Often language is a problem and the initial communication very difficult. If this is the case try to find someone who is fluent in their language to interpret for you. This can save many misunderstandings at a later date.

Before you leave a child with anyone you should know them well or at least have knowledge of them from a reliable source. The babysitter may be a local teenager or you may be part of a babysitting circle. Make sure that the babysitter knows where you are and has a contact number in case of emergency. Show them where everything is kept on their first visit – the kettle, the biscuit tin, the telephone and the fuse box. It is very helpful to be specific about bedtimes. When a child states that his normal bedtime is 11 pm and that he always has a bar of chocolate for supper, the babysitter should have the confidence to disagree.

It is a courtesy to warn anyone left with your children of potential problems such as sleepwalking or nightmares. The children should be told that the babysitter is in absolute charge. School-age babysitters may have homework to do and an early start in the morning. Try to be home when you say you will. Unless the babysitter has their own transport they should always be seen home at the end of the evening.

In return for the trust placed in them the babysitter should treat the home with respect. If they have consumed food or drink, the debris should be cleared away and the house should look much as it did when the parents went out.

Baby etiquette

Babies cannot be expected to follow rules of etiquette. They cry when they are hungry, make rude noises and are not always fragrant! It is a courtesy to the parent of a small baby to be considerate and tolerant towards the demands that this makes on them. Good friends may invite you to dinner and insist that you bring the baby. This can be very helpful in the early days but the parents should not presume that everyone present will want to share the baby's company all evening. Breastfeeding in public ultimately depends on how comfortable and relaxed the mother feels in the immediate situation. Many department stores now have mothers' rooms where they may feed and change their baby.

ENTERTAINING CHILDREN

Home for tea

Most children do, at some stage, want to invite a friend home for tea or to play for a few hours. It is an important step in expanding their horizons and a good opportunity for them to learn social skills at an early age. Sharing does not come easily to every child. It should be explained to them that visitors should be invited to play with their toys. Equally it may be necessary to ask the visitor to refrain from handling precious belongings too roughly. Don't be afraid to be firm. Children like to know their boundaries and if you make it clear from the beginning what is acceptable behaviour in your house it can deflect later problems.

Some children do not find it easy to eat unfamiliar food. If it is their first visit, it is worthwhile checking to see if there is anything which they are unable to eat.

Children's parties

When giving a children's party it is essential to know your limitations. If you are terribly houseproud, hold it in the garden or a local hall. If space is limited consider a cricket party in the local park or a trip to the swimming baths. Try to keep within a certain age group as it is very difficult to entertain children of widely differing ages. It may be worth considering an entertainer if the party seems a daunting prospect.

Most children's parties run from two to three hours. When making out the guest list remind the child that it is important to return hospitality even if they are not too keen to do so. Parents should bring their children promptly and then leave, unless they have been asked to stay.

The exception to this may be a toddler's party, when a parent would normally by invited. It is good manners to pick up your child on time and to make sure that nothing is left behind. The children may take home a piece of birthday cake or a balloon. Whether there is any kind of 'going home' gift really depends on the local custom. It is a good idea to collect all the birthday gifts together as the children arrive. This allows the child to greet her guests without being distracted by the opening of presents. Either save them until the party is over or open them at some stage of the party when a quiet moment is needed. It is a good time to teach the social art of saying thank you and looking pleased, even if three children have brought the same gift.

CHILDHOOD CELEBRATIONS

First communion

In the Roman Catholic Church a child makes his or her First Communion around the age of seven. This usually takes place during a morning mass and is often followed by a small party. Godparents may give the child a gift such as a prayer book to commemorate the event.

Confirmation
A child may be confirmed when his or her church recognizes that he has reached an acceptable level of maturity to make a Christian commitment. It is an occasion which involves the family and the parish as a whole. The baptismal godparents may be present or a witness or sponsor may accompany the child during the ceremony.

Bar mitzvah
This is an important ceremony which takes place when a Jewish boy reaches the age of thirteen. It takes place during the morning service on a Sabbath day and is usually followed by a celebratory banquet. The guests are invited formally to this and bring gifts.

BEHAVIOUR
Children have a highly developed sense of justice. 'It's not fair' is often used to sum up their feeling about life in general and parental behaviour in particular. And they can spot hypocrisy a mile away. There is no point on insisting on the niceties of etiquette – saying please and thank you, good table manners and consideration to other people – if they never witness such things at home. Good example may be an old-fashioned concept but it is a lot less painful than constant shouting and threats.

When children are misbehaving in public the parents' reaction may be to take the easy way out to avoid a scene. If you know that a confrontation may be likely i.e. a demand for sweets at the supermarket checkout, it is better to warn the child beforehand that this will not be possible. Critical remarks from other people are best ignored if you can manage to do so. Dealing with bad behaviour from other people's children is a difficult area. If it occurs when you have charge of them or they are in your house make it clear that you find it unacceptable. This is only fair to your own children who are expected to keep within certain norms of behaviour.

Try to deflect a situation whenever possible. It is better to ask if you may move a delicate piece of china than sweep up the pieces after your toddler had played football with it. Children can be totally oblivious to the noise they are making. If neighbours complain, apologies are better coming from the child than the parent. Appealing to their sense of fairness may help. Perhaps they can play indoors until a neighbour on nightshift has had his daytime sleep.

Teenagers
A good communications system between parents is invaluable throughout childhood and never more so than during teenage years. A teenager may pressurize a parent by insisting that 'everyone else is allowed to'. A few phone calls can easily verify this. On the other hand the child is also under a lot of pressure from his peers and it is not easy to stand out from the crowd. Whether you say yes or no to certain demands, always be prepared to discuss it. Talk to your child's friends as well as other parents and recognize that they must assume some responsibility for themselves in order to grow. Insisting that you know where they are going and who with looks more like concern and less like harassment if it is approached in the right way.

FRIENDS &
RELATIONSHIPS

Etiquette between friends and between partners in a relationship may sound formal but there are ground rules which keep friendships intact and sustain relationships.

Commonsense rules of courtship

Traditionally men were the wooers, women the wooed. That's no longer the case, but old habits die hard and many men and women still prefer traditional roles in courtship. But whoever issues the first invitation should take the responsibility for thinking of ways of spending the first 'date'. It might be a drink in a country pub, it might be a walk, but the initiator should suggest something even if this changes during discussion. There's nothing worse than being invited out and then being asked 'What would you like to do?' That kind of question deserves the response, 'Well first I'd like to slip over to Paris, dine at Maxim's then catch the Orient Express, lunch in Venice, take the private jet to Athens, watch the sun set over the Acropolis then move on to the South Pacific. . . .'

Whoever extends the invitation must also give some idea of what to expect, so that the guest knows what to wear (an over-dressed partner is a great turn off), whether to eat first and what the time scale will be.

Going Dutch

Travelling independently and paying your own way guarantees that you are under no obligation to the other person. Travelling independently is easy, paying less so. Waving your money around at box offices and in restaurants isn't a very tactful way of saying you'd like to go Dutch. Until you know each other better and can sort out who pays for what and when, you may have to play it by ear and wait until you can do it unobtrusively, or pay your way by reciprocal hospitality. Some men may be very put out by offers of going Dutch. Equally, some women may be very embarrassed if the man always insists on paying.

How to refuse an invitation

If you really don't want to go out with someone refuse firmly. Be polite but clear. Don't make excuses – they will sound as if you might be open to persuasion. You need not say why you don't want to go as the reason may be humiliating for the other person. Be brief – it always gets the message across. If someone becomes very persistent it may be impossible to avoid hurting his or her feelings, but if you have refused clearly enough such a situation doesn't usually occur.

If you would like to accept the invitation but have a previous engagement make it clear that this is the reason for your refusal, say that you would like to have gone and that you hope it can be arranged for another time.

Love is blind

If you get seriously involved with someone, don't do so at the expense of your friends. If you ignore them you'll lose them and no-one can afford to do that. Friends are constant in your life, the relationship may not be.

What sort of relationship?

In some ways the delicate area of forming a relationship was more clearly defined decades ago. The rules were more rigid – even heartbreaking, but expectations were clear. Today, different expectations from a relationship create a minefield. They can vary between friendship, sex, a non-exclusive relationship, an exclusive relationship, a relationship with commitment but without marriage, and marriage. Each partner may expect something quite different out of a relationship – a common cause of breaking up. The most practical and courteous course is to know your own mind and make clear your expectations. The worst thing you can do is to leave your partner guessing.

Sex or no sex?
Never lead anyone to expect that the relationship will be sexual if you are already sure that it won't be.

Breaking up is hard to do
Ending a relationship is never easy. If you have only been out with each other once or twice you can drop quietly out of the running – don't make contact, refuse all invitations. Ending a more regular relationship needs a more courageous approach; it is incredibly bad manners and cowardly to avoid it. However painful, it's best to be direct; the telephone can lead to misunderstandings as can letters. Meeting for a drink is probably the clearest way. The aim is to avoid hurting the other person; consideration for his or her feelings should be paramount. Ending a long-standing, serious relationship obviously needs lengthy discussion and explanation.

Close encounters of a difficult kind
Unwanted attentions can be very difficult to parry, especially if you are pursued or propositioned by a married woman or man, your partner's boss, a work colleague, a heterosexual if you are homosexual, someone you thought was just a friend or someone you simply don't fancy. Keep calm and give a low-key but very clear and polite refusal. Don't be too effusive or they may think that you want to be persuaded. If they persist and you already have a partner, suggest that the three of you go out together – that usually stops them. If you don't have a partner, make one up or call their bluff by saying that you'll bring a friend along – which can work wonders. If all that fails you may have to be direct to the point of rudeness, but that's a last resort.

If you spot a couple you know who technically shouldn't be together, don't jump to conclusions – their meeting is probably absolutely innocent. If you discover that your best friend's partner is having an affair, do not be tempted to interfere. Telling the friend may do more harm than good, especially if you are not aware of all the facts or circumstances. That said, each situation is different, and in certain circumstances it may be better to be open.

Etiquette between friends

Very formal manners between friends are unnecessary but courtesy, thoughtfulness and kindness enhance a friendship. If you meet friends in the street always introduce them to the group you are with, but don't muscle in on other people's friendships. If you are too pushy you will be rebuffed. Take it slowly and allow the friendship to develop naturally.

Paying your way

If a friend organizes tickets for a concert or the theatre remember to pay them. It can be very difficult for them to ask you for the money. If you are given hospitality at a friend's house but you don't cook, repay them by taking them out to a meal or to the theatre. Nothing is more irritating than a friend who always seems to arrive in the pub just as a round has been bought and doesn't offer to buy another until drinking-up time.

Borrowing and lending

Borrowing and lending can be a bone of contention too. People may seem very ready to lend you money, their car or their best ball gown, but unless you know them extremely well it's best not to borrow or lend. Some of the closest friendships have fallen apart over damaged or lost property. If you do borrow something, say how long you'll need it for and return it promptly.

Confidences

Friends will rely on you to keep their confidences. The surest way to lose a friend is to gossip about their private affairs.

Being a nuisance by not being a nuisance
Some family members and friends are so self-effacing
that they create trouble by trying not to be a nuisance.
When asked if they would like a cup of tea they reply
'Are you going to have one?' or 'Only if you're making
one, don't make one specially for me.' Such responses
are pointless; people do not offer a cup of tea unless they
are happy to make it.

Singles and couples
A single person can often feel like a gooseberry when
confronted with a couple. It is bad manners for a couple
to be exclusive and they should always do their best to
ensure that the single person is included in the conversation. Single people should not intrude into a
relationship.

Sharing a house or flat
Privacy, washing up and the telephone bill are the cause
of most arguments between flat-mates. Respect each
others privacy, don't go into other people's rooms
uninvited and certainly not when they are out. Never
borrow their clothes or other belongings without asking.
Have clear rules about household chores – it may seem
like school but rotas work best in the long run. Telephones are notoriously difficult to control. No-one ever
realizes how long they've been on the phone – it's
ALWAYS far longer than you think. Pay phones elimi-
nate the problem but are expensive to install. You can
get a timing device, which is cheaper. Log each call as
you make it. If you are irritated by someone's behaviour,
don't brood on it. Work out whether you are being
reasonable, if you are, speak directly to the friend
concerned before the irritation has driven you to a
frenzy.

Family privacy
If you are legally an adult you can lead your own life and
your parents should respect your privacy. However, if

you are still living at home, respect the views of your parents whilst in their house.

Separation and divorce

Don't expect everyone to hear on the grapevine that you have separated or divorced. Tell your family, friends and relevant neighbours and colleagues. If you have children tell all adults with whom they come into contact, especially teachers. This may appear to be making a painful and private matter too public, but you and your friends will feel worse if they innocently put their foot in it. Friends will also want to offer comfort and practical support.

Taking sides

It's almost impossible for friends not to take sides, but they should do everything to avoid aggravating the situation. After the break, friends should not be tempted into playing games by inviting both parties to a social gathering. If, as a friend, you genuinely want to ask them both, 'phone them individually and explain that the ex-partner may be there and then they have the choice of whether to attend or not. Family occasions can be more tricky, but if both parties attend the same function they should never continue the battle in public.

Of course many divorced couples remain friends for their own and the children's sakes, and even if the couple find it difficult to see each other they often wish to remain friends with their in-laws. If either party re-marries they should tell their ex-partner and in-laws as soon as possible.

Forms of address

A woman who changed her name on marrying can go back to her single name whenever she likes as long as she informs the bank, etc., and changes her name on all legal documents. She can keep her married name if she prefers. Children of a divorced couple usually keep the father's name.

VISITORS AT HOME & STAYING WITH FRIENDS

AT HOME

Uninvited guests

Dropping in on someone can give them a delightful surprise or an awful shock. It may be an inopportune moment – they are in the bath, having a family row, just about to sit down to a meal, in which case your visit may be embarrassing. To preserve their dignity and privacy and your friendship it's advisable to telephone first and ask if you may call and when.

If you are the victim of an unexpected visit at an inconvenient moment try to look sufficiently pleased so that the visitor will not be offended, but not so pleased that they will not take the hint and leave. Most friends will be sensitive enough to realize that it is not a good moment. If visitors are insensitive and insist on coming in, you may have to resort to the little white lie, 'How lovely to see you but I'm afraid I was just about to go out, perhaps you will be able to come round another day. May I give you a ring and we'll arrange a time?' You may have to resort to the same sort of white lie if someone arrives and outstays their welcome (though washing up the tea cups usually works!). Some people are notoriously insensitive to others and an elegant white lie is sometimes the only way to get out of a difficult situation.

HOSPITAL VISITS

When visiting a patient in hospital note that times and numbers of visitors are often stipulated by the hospital, but if there are no regulations make your visit short and sweet, unless the invalid asks you to stay longer. Streams of visitors can be very exhausting; bedside parties are often more enjoyable for the visitors than for the sick. If there are already several visitors at the bedside, wait outside until the crush has subsided. If someone is seriously ill it is advisable to 'phone the hospital or a close friend or relative and ask if it is a good idea to visit.

Flowers are nearly always welcome whatever the sex of the recipient. Luxurious fruit, magazines and books are also acceptable, but the most important things of all is your presence. Do not stay away because you feel that you can't do anything. In most cases hospital visitors boost morale and aid recovery.

WEEKENDS AWAY

The host
If you are inviting close friends for the weekend they will know what to expect, but a first time visitor will need some help from you when you give the invitation. Make the invitation clear, suggest a time of arrival – in time for Friday dinner or Saturday lunch, and tell your guests what sort of events to expect so that they can pack suitable clothes. They may be miffed at missing the hunt ball because they've only packed wellies and sweaters. Give them an idea of when you expect them to depart by saying something like, 'I do hope you'll be able to stay for Sunday lunch.'

When guests arrive, show them to their rooms. You will, of course, have made up the beds and put out fresh towels. You can also put flowers, mineral water, a radio, books and magazines in the room. Someone we know even provides biscuits for a midnight nibble. Show them where the bathroom is and if it's not en suite, give them some idea of who else will be using it so that your guests can judge when to get up. Be clear about the time of breakfast – it's terribly embarrassing to come down half-an-hour after everyone else has started.

Children are often shy of visitors at first and then won't leave them alone. Encourage them to be friendly but discourage them from bouncing over the guest's bed at 6 am in the morning.

The guest
You may want to arrive bearing gifts. That's fine if you know your hosts well, but if you don't it may be wiser to wait until the visit is over, when you will have more idea of their needs and tastes. 'Make yourself at home', hardly ever means just that. If you are new to a house be circumspect. Don't put your feet up on the sofa or coffee table; work out which is the host's favourite chair and avoid it; don't spend hours in the only bathroom; and don't grab the popular bits of the Sunday paper and hog them for the morning.

The best guests are game to join in the weekend's activities and to offer help without being interfering. You will, of course, make your own bed, clean out the bath and basin when you've used them and do useful chores like laying the table. You can pray that they have a dishwasher but if they don't, wipe up cheerfully. You won't be asked again if you put your feet up in front of the telly while everyone else is in the kitchen.

Paying your way
Ask before you use the telephone. If you have to make a long distance or an international call arrange with the operator to tell you how much it cost and leave the money beside the telephone. Your host may feel too embarrassed to accept if you offer money, so just leave it unobtrusively.

You can also pay for outings while you are away. Don't get locked into arguments over who pays. If the host is adamant that you should not pay, then wait and see if there is another opportunity. If one doesn't arise, you can always buy a good bottle of wine to go with a meal.

Staff
If the house is grand enough to have staff they will probably unpack for you and look after you while you are there. It's quite correct to leave them a tip at the end

of the visit. If you aren't certain how much, ask your host. Don't take presents or offer to pay for outings or buy wine when you visit such a household.

Two beds or not two beds?
This is a question which you may have to ask if an unmarried couple who don't live together comes to stay. If they don't tell you outright when you invite them you will have to ask (unless of course you disapprove and automatically put them in separate rooms). One friend got round this awkward little moment by asking, 'One pair of sheets or two?'

As a guest it is a breach of hospitality to hop into your girl/boyfriend's bed if you have been put in separate rooms. You may consider it stuffy and moralizing but when staying in someone's house you should abide by the host's wishes. As a host, it is only courteous to give one room to a couple in an established relationship.

Petiquette
Not everyone loves your dog or cat as much as you do and they certainly won't want your huge alsatian bounding over their new carpet when you drop in for tea. You should avoid taking your dog on visits. If it has to be with you, leave it in the car. You should only ask if you may bring the dog into a house where you know it will be welcome, and the same applies to travelling cats. If you invite guests to say for the weekend warn them if you have pets as they may be allergic to them, especially to cats. Train your dog not to jump up at people, it can be very disconcerting for people who are not used to them.

INVITATIONS & LETTERS

In spite of the popularity of the telephone, the written word still has an important place in modern etiquette. A written invitation remains the norm for many social occasions. It has the great advantage of removing the possibility of confusion over dates and times. It serves as a reminder of the event and the sender can keep a check on numbers.

At home, the 'At Home' card is still used for some parties and traditionally bears the name of the hostess only:

Mr & Mrs Mark Walker

Mrs Cecil Dibbs
at home
Friday 8 August 19—

RSVP
Chase Cottage,
Studland Avenue,
Peterborough.

6.30-8.30pm

If the event is not to take place at home – for instance a supper dance at a hotel – the invitation might ask for 'the pleasure of your company'. If the invitation is for a particular occasion this should be indicated.

The guests' names are written at the top left hand corner of the invitation. For close friends and relations, simply put their christian names.

It should be made clear from the wording the exact nature of the event. Often the time will indicate whether it is an invitation for drinks or whether food will be served. If a guest is still not sure it is quite in order to make a telephone call enquiring about eating arrangements. Nothing is worse than being expected to eat another meal when you have already eaten at home!

A prompt response to an invitation is not only courteous but necessary, especially where caterers are involved.

If the invitation was extended informally on the telephone, it is a good idea to send a reminder card with date and time nearer the event.

WEDDING INVITATIONS

The standard form of invitation to a wedding is worded as follows:

Mr & Mrs Gareth Thomas

Mr & Mrs Arthur Blake
request the pleasure
of your company
at the marriage of their daughter
Abigail Louise
to
Mr Anthony David Lowe
at St Benedict's Church, Hayes
on Saturday 4 February at 11.30 am
and afterwards at the Berkeley Hotel, Hayes.

6 Shelley Avenue, Hayes,
Middlesex.

If the bridegroom has a title such as Doctor or Major this is included in the invitation.

Sometimes an invitation will be for either the service or the reception only. An invitation for the latter would read:

Mr & Mrs Gareth Thomas

Mr & Mrs Arthur Blake
request the pleasure of your company at
the reception to follow the marriage of
their daughter
Abigail Louise
to
Mr Anthony David Lowe
At the Berkeley Hotel, Hayes
Saturday, 4 February at 1pm.

6, Shelley Avenue,
Hayes,
Middlesex   *R S V P*

When the invitation is for the ceremony only, the standard form is used, omitting the words 'and afterwards at' etc.

Not all invitations can be covered by this formula. Printers or stationers can usually advise on any variations which might be necessary for your particular circumstances.

Weddings are not always hosted by the bride's parents. In such cases, the wording might be adapted as follows:

Mr & Mrs Andrew Field
request the pleasure of the company of

Mr & Mrs Jeremy Jones

at the marriage of their niece
Moira
to
Mr James Mann
at St Mary's, Clapham
on Saturday 27 October at 11.30am
and afterwards at the Englewood Hotel, Clapham

57 Thurleston Avenue,
Clapham,
London SW12.

RSVP

In the case of divorced parents invitations would normally come from the bride's mother. If the mother has remarried both her surname and that of her daughter should be included. Where the bride lives with her father and he has remarried, the invitation is sent by the father and his new wife.

In the case of a second marriage the invitation is still sent by the parents if the bride is young. Otherwise a close friend or the bride herself can send them.

Not all invitations can be covered by these examples. Printers or stationers can usually advise on any variations which might be necessary.

REPLYING TO INVITATIONS

The general rule is to reply as promptly as possible. If there is a good reason to delay your decision to attend, such as ill health, it is courteous to let the host/hostess know this. An acceptance by phone will often suffice but in the case of more formal occasions written confirmation should be sent. These are written in the third person e.g.

Yew Tree Lodge,
Lewes,
Sussex.

Mr & Mrs David King thank Mr & Mrs Ferrier for their kind invitation to the wedding of their daughter, Clare, on Saturday 9 November and have great pleasure in accepting.

Should the invitation have to be declined a reason should be given, e.g.:

Yew Tree Lodge,
Lewes,
Sussex.

Mr & Mrs David King thank Mr & Mrs Ferrier for their kind invitation to the marriage of their daughter Clare on Saturday 9 November but regret that they are unable to accept because of a previous engagement.

In order to make this seem less formal a note could be added wishing the couple every happiness.

Replies to invitations should be addressed to all the names on the invitation card, not just to one of them.

Sometimes a single person is invited to bring a guest. When replying, it is good manners to tell the host/hostess if another person will be coming and say who they are.

When an invitation has a telephone number beneath the RSVP a telephone confirmation is fine. This is the moment to ask any questions which may be worrying you regarding gifts or dress, for example.

Never turn up at a party with an uninvited guest unless you have the permission of the host.

Declining an invitation can sometimes be difficult. If the invitation comes by telephone and you wish to have more time to consider it you could say that you need to consult your diary. It is not very polite to give a casual, 'I'll think about it', sort of response.

Royal invitations

Invitations from the Queen or Queen Mother are treated as commands. The acceptance may read as follows:

> *Mr & Mrs Gordon McBride thank Mr _____, private secretary to Her Majesty for the invitation to the garden party and have the honour to accept Her Majesty's command at Buckingham Palace at 2.30 pm on 6 June.*

The reply should be handwritten. Invitations from other members of the Royal Family are replied to in the usual way.

LETTER WRITING

Although letter writing is less common today than in the past there are times when it cannot be avoided. Sometimes it is much easier to put thoughts down on paper than to meet someone face to face.

Pen and paper

Unless you are writing a business letter or your handwriting is totally illegible, letters should be written by hand. If you have to type a letter 'topping and tailing' at least should be in your own handwriting. Today there is a great variety of coloured and patterned writing paper available. It really depends on the nature of your correspondence as to which style you use. A letter of sympathy, for example, would look out of place on pink striped paper. When in doubt it is best to stick to white or blue.

In the beginning

The usual style of opening a letter is 'Dear____'. Obviously letters to loved ones may begin in a more affectionate way. Forms of address for those with titles are given at the end of the chapter.

At the end

For business correspondence 'Yours faithfully' is the correct way to end your letter. 'Yours sincerely' or 'Yours truly' are used for many other letters. A variety of affectionate terms are employed for letters to close friends and family. It really is up to the writer and depends on the level of intimacy with the person to whom they are writing.

When to write

Letters of thanks or congratulation should be written as close to the event as possible. These may be brief and to the point. Sometimes a short note can express more than a long-winded letter. Letters to older people or those who cannot get about very much will be appreciated.

These can be as long as you like and full of information about what you have been doing so that the recipient feels that they are in touch with the world.

Postcards

It is a good idea to keep a stock of postcards, perhaps collected from museums and galleries. Not only are these a pleasure to receive but the lack of space keeps wording brief. They are especially effective when used by those with a witty turn of phrase. More formally printed correspondence cards with the name and address of the sender at the top are also useful for brief accompanying notes.

Letters of sympathy and condolence are dealt with more fully on page 94. These are perhaps the hardest letters of all to write. It is helpful to mention that you do not expect a reply.

Letters of complaint, enquiry or confirmation

These are normally set out as business letters, and are generally typed, with the name and address of the person to whom you are writing placed at the top left hand of the page above the greeting.

It is not a good idea to write a letter of complaint in the heat of the moment. Keep the letter brief and to the point. Icy politeness is a lot more effective than a tirade of abuse! If you receive a letter of complaint your response will depend on whether you think that it is justified or not. If your dog, for example, has trampled all over an allotment, a swift letter of apology can do much to diffuse the situation. The written word can be a very powerful means of putting your opinion across to another person, so do make sure that your letter reflects exactly what you feel and that there is no room for ambiguity.

Hotels and travel agencies sometimes ask for a letter of confirmation of a booking. These may be written as follows:

25 Park Road,
Bramhall,
Cheshire

Mrs Humble,
The Grange Hotel,
Weymouth,
Dorset.

Dear Mrs Humble,　　　　*23 June 19—*

　Further to our telephone conversation this afternoon, I confirm my reservation for a double room with bath for the week beginning 22 August. My estimated time of arrival will be around 4 pm. I enclose a deposit as requested.

Yours sincerely,
Roger Brown

The right address

The address should be written on the lower half of the envelope. This is not a demand of etiquette but to avoid the address becoming obliterated by the franking machine. 'Esquire' is not used very often – it traditionally denoted someone who owned land. Mr, Mrs, Miss or Ms are the usual forms of address but we sometimes have occasion to write to someone who does not fall into these categories. This table shows some forms of address that you might need.

Forms of address

	Envelopes	*Opening of letter*
Royalty and aristocracy		
The Queen	'The Private Secretary to Her Majesty the Queen'	Dear Sir or Madam (depending on the private secretary)
Duke of Edinburgh	Procedure as above	As above
Queen Mother	Procedure as above	As above
A Royal Prince	His Royal Highness The Prince Edward	Your Royal Highness
A Royal Princess	Her Royal Highness, The Princess of Wales	Your Royal Highness
A Royal Duke	His Royal Highness, The Duke of Gloucester	Your Royal Highness
A Royal Duchess	Her Royal Highness, The Duchess of York	Your Royal Highness
Duke	The Duke of Mendip	Dear Duke
Duchess	The Duchess of Mendip	Dear Duchess
Earl	The Earl of Clavelly	Dear Lord Clavelly
Countess	The Countess of Deal	Dear Lady Deal
Baron	The Lord St Ives	Dear Lord St Ives
Baron's wife	The Lady St Ives	Dear Lady St Ives
Knight	Sir Arthur Hicks	Dear Sir Arthur
Knight's wife	Lady Hicks	Dear Lady Hicks
Untitled people		
Men	Mr Harold Eves	Dear Mr Eves
Married women	Mrs Harold Eves	Dear Mrs Eves
Widows	Mrs Harold Eves	Dear Mrs Eves
Divorcees	Mrs Sheila Eves	Dear Mrs Eves

Many women choose to use their own name after marriage or prefer the prefix Ms. A useful rule of thumb is to address them in the manner in which they sign themselves.

Government

The Prime Minster	The Rt. Hon. Margaret Thatcher, P.C., M.P. (unofficial)	
	The Prime Minister (official)	Dear Prime Minister
Chancellor of the Exchequer	The Rt. Hon. Percy Mann, P.C., M.P. (unofficial)	
	The Chancellor of the Exchequer (official)	Dear Chancellor
Secretaries of State	The Foreign Secretary	Dear Secretary of State or Dear Foreign Secretary
M.P.s	Michael Peach, Esq. M.P.	Dear Mr Peach

The law

High Court Judge	The Hon. Mr Justice Bright	Dear Judge
Woman High Court Judge	The Hon. Mrs Justice Finch	(Dear) Madam
Circuit Court Judges	His Honour Judge Morris	(Dear) Sir
Queen's Counsel	Fergus Brown, Esq. Q.C.	Dear Mr Brown

The clergy
Church of England

Archbishop	The Most Reverend and Rt. Hon. the Lord Archbishop of Canterbury	Dear Archbishop
Bishop	The Right Reverend the Bishop of Durham	Dear Bishop
Vicar	The Reverend Andrew Wright	Dear Mr Wright

Jewish

Rabbis	Rabbi J. Blue	Dear Rabbi Blue
Ministers	The Reverend Jacob Blue	Dear Mr Blue

Roman Catholic

The Pope	His Holiness the Pope	Your Holiness
Cardinals	His Eminence the Cardinal Archbishop of Westminster	Dear Cardinal Brown
Bishops	The Right Reverend John Carr, Bishop of Maryland	My Lord Bishop
Priests	The Reverend James Swan	Dear Father Swan

Local government

Lord Mayor or Lady Mayor	The Right Worshipful the Lord Mayor	Dear Lord Mayor (social official) My Lord Mayor (formal official)
Lady Mayoress	The Lady Mayoress of Richmond	As above but Mayoress
Councillor	Councillor Mrs Jones (official) By name (social)	Dear Councillor

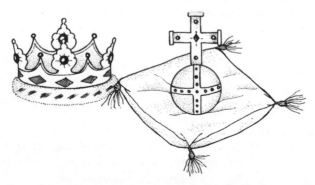

FORMAL OCCASIONS

ROYALTY

The Royal Family attend a great many functions and charity events throughout the year and are introduced to hundreds of people. There is a possibility that you may find yourself in a situation which involves meeting royalty. This should not cause any undue anxiety. Expert guidance is always available and advice given readily as to protocol on such occasions. In this chapter we will be looking at the most common worries as well as specific occasions.

Meeting royalty

It is usual for a woman to curtsy and a man to bow on being introduced. The curtsy should not be elaborate but it is a good idea to practise if you want to avoid losing your balance. Keep your head up and your back straight and you should have no problems. Although royalty should always initiate conversation, etiquette is a little less formal than in the past. It is in order today to ask a question or to bring up a subject – but these should obviously be of a non-provocative nature.

The Queen and the Queen Mother are addressed initially as 'Your Majesty' and thereafter as 'Ma'am' (to rhyme with jam). A royal Prince or Princess is addressed as 'Your Highness' and subsequently as 'Sir' or 'Ma'am'. In a formal speech, references to you or your are replaced with 'Your Majesty' or 'Your Royal Highness'. When introducing someone to royalty one would say 'Your Royal Highness, may I introduce you to Miss Ruth Barker?'

Royal invitations (see page 61)

All royal invitations come with full details regarding the event. This will include dress, car parking, directions and any other information which you might need. If you have any queries a phone call to the relevant secretary should set your mind at rest.

Garden parties

The invitation to a Royal Garden Party will include an admission card which must be taken with you on the day. If you are unable to accept the invitation the admission card must be returned.

Dress Women wear afternoon dresses, often with a hat. Men may wear morning coats or lounge suits, official dress or uniform. National dress may be worn by men and women. As this is an outside event it is a good idea to take an umbrella or some kind of outer wear if the weather looks uncertain. Cameras are not allowed.

Time Guests may enter from 3.15 pm, although the Royal party does not arrive until 4 pm. Some present-ations may be made before the royal group mixes informally with the guests. As they move around a path is made for them to move freely. Tea is served to the guests in tents separate from the royal party. The occasion is brought to an end by the National Anthem at 6 pm. It is possible to leave before the Royal Party but, as the event is quite short, this rarely happens in practice.

Investitures

The ceremony itself does not take much longer than an hour. Everyone concerned is well-briefed beforehand so there is no need to be anxious.

Dress is much the same as for a garden party although women's hats should be small so as not to obscure the view of other guests. Photographs may be taken outside the palace.

Banquets

These are given in honour of a visiting head of state. Invitations come with presentation cards – both of which must be brought to the occasion.

Dress Men wear white tie or national dress. Women

wear long dresses or national dress. Jewelry may be very formal. Now is your chance to wear the family tiara!

At every stage of the event, the guests are ushered into the correct place by members of the royal household. Following a formal presentation, each guest finds his place at table and stands behind his or her chair until the Royal Party is seated. After dinner the Queen makes a speech of welcome to the guest of honour and proposes a toast to them. The visiting Head of State then makes a speech and concludes with the loyal toast. The guests stand for both toasts, drink, and sit down again. Nobody should leave before the National Anthem at the end of the evening, when the Royal Party leaves.

State Opening of Parliament
If you are invited to the Royal Gallery to watch the procession, women should wear a day dress and a small hat and men a morning or lounge suit or service dress.

Royal Ascot
Tickets for the Royal Enclosure must be applied for and require a sponsor. There are very strict rules of etiquette regarding dress, and if they are not followed you may be refused entry.
Dress Women wear formal day dresses and a hat and men wear morning coats. Cameras are not allowed.

Henley Royal Regatta
Admission to the Stewards' Enclosure is by invitation only.
Dress Men must wear jackets with either a tie or cravat. Sports jackets or club blazers are fine. Caps or boaters may be worn where appropriate.

Women wear day dresses and, if they wish to, hats. Trousers may not be worn by women, no matter how smart they are.

DIPLOMATIC OCCASIONS
Protocol is very strict in diplomatic circles. This serves a

very important purpose as it reduces the risk of offence where religious, social and political persuasions differ.

Ambassadors of foreign countries or High Commissioners of Commonwealth countries have precedence according to their length of service.

Dress may vary between Embassies and it is best to check what is permissible before the event.

Receptions may be held at an Embassy or at a hotel. The invitation will state the reason for the reception and all the necessary information. Replies are written in the third person. If the invitation states that dress is informal this means a lounge suit for a man and a day dress for a woman. Dress formal will indicate black or white tie. If it states that 'Decorations will be worn' then the correct dress will be white tie. It is useful to do some homework before attending a diplomatic occasion as codes of behaviour do vary between countries.

FORMAL DINNERS
These may include civic dinners or dinners given by the universities or armed services.

High table
There is usually a High Table at a formal dinner or banquet. It is possible that those who will sit at the high table enter when everyone is seated. This may be accompanied by clapping but if you are unsure do wait until someone else has started to clap.

If a rose bowl or finger bowl is passed around the table rinse your fingers and dry them on your napkin.

Port is passed to the left and never drunk before the loyal toast (which may be drunk in port).

Toasts
Don't be too quick to leap to your feet – not all toasts are drunk standing up. The navy, for example, drinks the loyal toast ('The Queen') sitting down. If you are not sure how a toast will be drunk, the rule is to watch and

wait and to do what everyone else does. It is quite all right to drink a toast in water or a soft drink if you do not drink alcohol.

Smoking

It is not usual to smoke until after the loyal toast. If there is no toast an announcement will be made.

If coffee and liqueurs are to be served in another room it is better to wait until then. On occasions when the ladies retire to another room, it is usually permissible to smoke when they have left.

ETIQUETTE AND THE ARTS

Some entertainments and performances are more formal than others and it is wise to know what to expect. Considerate behaviour at any sort of performance should include the following:

Punctuality It is a courtesy to the performers as well as to the rest of the audience to be in good time. In many instances you will not be allowed into the auditorium until the end of an act or in some cases not until the interval.

Taking your seat Many older theatres and concert halls have very little room between the rows of seats. If someone needs to get to their seat it is courteous to stand to let them pass, picking up any bags and umbrellas which may be in the way. If somebody stands up for you, a quiet thankyou is in order – especially if you are late and everyone else is seated. It sometimes happens that you find someone is sitting in your seat. Usually a comparison of tickets will sort out the problem. If, however, the person refuses to budge, find a member of the house staff to arbitrate rather than starting to argue.

Keeping quiet Talking during a performance is obviously very bad manners but it is amazing how many people whisper very loudly and seem to think that no-one can hear them! The most annoying people of all are those who feel they have to explain the plot or guess the ending. Critical comments should be saved for the interval. Wrapping papers, eating apples and persistent sniffing particularly during quiet moments should be avoided. Snores from people who have fallen asleep can be deflected with a gentle nudge.

First nights Today few people dress up to go to the theatre. The exception to this is a First Night. This tends to be a dressier occasion with many celebrities present in the audience. Gala performances which may take place in the presence of royalty also require more formal dress.

Applause Do be quite sure that the act has come to an end before you start to applaud. In most productions this may be quite obvious by a lighting change or a curtain. If in doubt – wait. Sometimes there is a burst of applause when a particularly well-known or well-liked actor comes onto the stage. This is generally not a good idea as it can interrupt the flow of the action. It is better to save special applause for a particular performer until he or she takes their bow at the end.

Many theatres have their own conventions regarding the number of curtain calls to take. There is usually a very clear feeling when the last bow has been taken and it is pointless to go on applauding after this. If the house lights have come up it is courteous to remain in your seat until the applause is finished. No actor enjoys watching an audience leaving in droves as they take their curtain call.

Opera and ballet As well as applauding at the end of each act it is acceptable to applaud a fine aria or a solo dance in the middle of a scene. At the end of an opera, shouts of 'Bravo' may follow a good performance. This is the only thing which should be shouted. Cries of 'smashing' or 'play it again, Sam,' are not acceptable.

If you are moved to stand up whilst applauding, either at the theatre or the opera, do have the courage of your convictions. It looks rather feeble if you sit down again as soon as you realize that you are the only one standing.

It is a chance you have to take. At any musical performance where an encore may be taken, you should sit down again whilst this is performed.

Recitals and concerts Some of the strictest rules of etiquette apply to applause at these events. During a lieder recital, for example, applause is given at the end of a sequence of songs. The programme will indicate where these pauses occur. If you are following the English translation in your programme or score you should not turn the page in the middle of a song but wait until it has ended.

At the performance of a symphony there is no applause between movements. At these events as well as at the opera and ballet applause should be held back until the music has died away completely.

Covent Garden Except at a gala performance where the dress is usually black tie, there are no set rules of dress. Generally speaking the style of dress reflects the cost of the seats. The boxes have waiter service at the interval.

Glyndebourne This opera house is worth a special mention as it does have traditions of its own. Set in the grounds of a manor house at Lewes in Sussex, performances take place during the summer months. The programme begins early (around 5 pm, depending on the length of the opera). This is to allow for the long interval of seventy minutes during which the audience have their dinner. This may be eaten in the restaurant but, more traditionally, (and much more fun) many people bring a picnic and eat it by the lake.

Glyndebourne picnics are quite special. It is wise to get there early and set up the picnic in the place of your choice. You will need to bring all your cutlery and picnic furniture and there is great variation in formality. Anything may be produced from a simple travelling rug to a linen covered table complete with silver service.

Dress is black tie for men and long or ballerina length dresses for women.

WHAT TO WEAR

'The consciousness of being perfectly dressed may bestow a peace such as religion cannot give,' said Herbert Spencer. Wearing the right clothes for the occasion puts everyone at ease. It isn't just a matter of clothes either: turning up in your jeans and sweatshirt at a special celebration shows a lack of appreciation for all the effort the host has put into the party. Acceptable dress is very flexible today, but there are still times when certain forms of dress are more appropriate than others, particularly if the occasion is formal.

FORMAL MENSWEAR

Many men hire formal wear because it is worn so infrequently, although it is not unusual to own a dinner jacket. Good hire firms are experts on the correct dress for the occasion and will ensure that you have the right outfit. They will also advise on accessories such as shoes and on the wearing of decorations, orders and medals. If you need to hire formal wear order it in plenty of time, especially if it is for a public occasion such as Royal Ascot. Don't expect the hire company to be able to give you a perfect fit of a suit at 5.30 pm the day before it's needed.

Morning dress

Morning dress is usually hired and worn on formal occasions such as weddings, Royal Ascot and investitures. It consists either of a black morning coat, striped trousers and a black top hat, or a grey jacket and matching trousers and a grey top hat which is often worn at weddings. Wear morning dress with a stiff-collared white shirt, silver tie, black shoes (oxfords, not slip-ons) and black socks. Waistcoats should be fawn or pale beige with a black coat, and grey with a grey coat. If you wish to carry gloves, grey are correct with a grey suit and yellow chamois with a black suit.

Black tie

When an invitation says 'black tie' it means dinner jacket and bow tie. The invitation will usually be for a formal dinner or dance. The dinner jacket and matching trousers may be hired. The suit is usually black (although very dark blue is sometimes worn). The jacket frequently has silk or braided lapels and is tail-less. It may be single or double breasted according to the fashion of the moment. The trousers are sometimes braided down the outside leg. Dinner jackets are worn with a decorative shirt, traditionally white with a pique or pleated front.

Bow ties are also subject to fashion. Traditionally they are black silk but velvet and bright colours or patterns in silk are also worn, especially by young men. You can wear a matching silk cummerbund with a single-breasted suit; there's no point if the suit is double-breasted or has a waistcoat since it won't show. Black shoes and socks are worn, but your socks can defy convention if you are brave or young and be scarlet to match your bow tie. In the tropics or on summer evenings a white dinner jacket can look very debonair. Wear it with black trousers.

White tie

'White tie' is full evening dress and is reserved for very formal occasions, usually balls. The invitation will say whether it is required. Most people hire full evening dress, which consists of a black tail coat and matching trousers, a stiff, pique-fronted shirt, a separate wing collar, a white pique bow tie and matching waistcoat. The bow tie is rarely of the clip on variety, so practise tying it before the great day. The shirt is fastened with decorative studs, not buttons, which are often gold or mother-of-pearl. If you hire the suit studs are usually included but cufflinks are often not and they are needed for the dress shirt and should match the studs as closely as possible. If you are lucky you may have a set of antique studs and matching cufflinks. Shoes should really be black patent leather pumps but elegant patent lace-ups are frequently worn.

DECORATIONS AND MEDALS

Decorations and medals are sometimes worn on formal occasions. The invitation will say if they are appropriate, so don't wear them if it doesn't.

On 'white tie' occasions, Knights wear the ribbon and badge of the most senior British chivalric order to which they belong. They wear a foreign order if that is more appropriate to the occasion. Stars (up to four) are worn on the left breast together with a neck badge which hangs from a miniature ribbon just below the bow tie. Miniature orders, decorations and medals are worn on a medal bar. The Order of Merit, the Thistle, the Garter, the Companion of Honour and the Baronet's Badge are worn, but not in miniature.

On 'black tie' occasions wear miniatures on a bar on the left breast of the jacket. One star and one neck badge on a miniature ribbon may also be worn.

It is very rare to wear decorations and medals with morning dress but if necessary they should be worn as for white tie. Full-size decorations, medals and orders are worn on a bar on the left side of the jacket.

Decorations and medals worn just with a suit is a situation that usually occurs at Remembrance Sunday services and parades. Full-size medals are worn on the left breast of the jacket. Badges and stars are not worn but a neck badge may be.

OTHER MENSWEAR

Suits

If you work in a formal office you will probably be

expected to wear a suit. Suits are also worn to weddings, formal dinners and receptions. Dark suits in navy or charcoal grey are worn on formal occasions, lighter colours and brown in more relaxed situations. According to fashion and taste suits may be single or double-breasted and may or may not have a matching waistcoat. To avoid looking like a concertina undo the bottom button of a double-breasted suit when you sit down. Single-breasted suits can also look rumpled when you sit, especially if you appear on television. Undo the middle button (the only one you should ever fasten) and do it up when you stand again. Jackets should not be removed at formal functions unless the occasion slides into informality. Leave the bottom button of a waistcoat unfastened. The sleeves of a jacket should allow half an inch of shirt cuff to show. Don't put pens in the top outside pocket of a jacket. Ideally, pens and wallet go in the inside breast pocket but this may not be wise if you take your jacket off in the office and leave it unattended.

Ties
Club, regimental and old school ties should only be worn by genuine members. If you adopt the tie of an organization with which you have no connection you may be asked many questions about people you do not know which could be extremely embarrassing.

Hats
Hats are rarely worn in town, except in extremely cold weather. In the country they are more popular. A man should never wear a hat indoors.

Shoes
Wear shoes that are appropriate to the circumstances. Smart town shoes, designed to be worn with a suit look out of place in the country or with jeans. Wear thin-soled shoes for dancing and pale or rope-soled shoes on the deck of a boat to avoid marking it. Don't wear brown shoes with a dark grey or navy suit.

WOMENSWEAR

Dress for women is now far less rigid than it is for men. Today, judging the formality of the function can be a problem for there is nothing worse than being either under or over dressed for the occasion. Most hosts will indicate what sort of dress is expected and it's perfectly correct to ask for some guidance if they don't.

What to wear if the invitation says 'white tie'
A long dress or a two-piece in a rich fabric is the correct accompaniment for a white tie occasion. White tie is reserved for very formal occasions and ball gowns and jewels, if you have them, should be worn.

What to wear if the invition says 'black tie'
Wear a long or short dress or two-piece in a decorative material if the occasion is 'black tie'. Evening trousers may also be worn, but these are more prone to the vagaries of fashion. The choice depends on the fashion of the moment and the preference and age of the assembled company. If it is a company dinner dance at a rather smart hotel and you are uncertain whether to wear long or short seek the advice of someone who attends the function regularly.

What to wear if the invitation says morning dress
Wear a smart day dress or suit in a fashionable but acceptable length. Extremely short skirts may shock if you wear them at a very formal function, so steer clear of them. Hats are often worn and can really transform an outfit.

Gloves
Gloves sometimes accompany the sort of smart outfit worn to a wedding. Evening gloves are rarely worn today, but on very formal occasions such as state functions they may be. Wear long evening gloves with sleeveless or short sleeved dresses. Keep them on for introductions and dancing, remove them when eating.

BUSINESS ETIQUETTE

Although work and social etiquette are different in detail their aim is the same: to create an atmosphere where people are at their best, where they feel confident and natural.

YOU AND YOUR BOSS

The degree of informality between you and your boss will depend on the type of work in which you are involved and the character of the person in charge. If it is a formal office your boss may expect you to use his or her surname. Don't presume that you may use christian names unless it is obviously office practice or the boss asks you to.

Get your duties clearly defined from the beginning. A good job description is important as there can then be no confusion or argument over your work load and duties.

Bosses are not infallible and you may disagree with them. That's perfectly all right but pick carefully the time, place and manner in which you give your opinion. Be polite and never disagree in front of clients or visitors.

If you feel that your boss is making unreasonable demands on your time (it might be taken for granted that a secretary should stop work and make tea for example), ask to see him/her to explain your grievance before you get to the point of wanting to empty the tea pot over them. Do not moan about it to someone else or go to a more senior member of staff behind your boss's back.

Don't be amazed or outraged if your boss doesn't say please or thank you for every little thing you do. Stopping for the niceties of etiquette would interrupt the work flow too much, but mutual respect and courtesy are essential to an efficient working atmosphere.

It is both professional and polite to ask your boss if

EDINBURGH BOOKSHOP

ORDER NO.   127100

07063000   WARD LOCK LTD.

070636417   SEDDON / GILD...

MODERN ETIQUET...

C

DATE ORDER PLACED 291288   DE...

4

PAPER

you may have time off to go to the doctor, attend a funeral or wait for the plumber to arrive. Some bosses were in the wrong queue when compassion and understanding were handed out. You are not a missionary so don't try to convert them; explain the situation, if they refuse say, politely but equally firmly, that you will be keeping the appointment. If there is still difficulty and you have a good personnel department explain the situation to them and let them deal with it.

YOU AND YOUR STAFF

When did you last thank someone who works for you? Staff who are shown consideration usually work more willingly than those who are not. The degree of feedback in terms of work is in direct relation to the way in which staff are managed and that includes courtesy.

Many bosses make unreasonable and thoughtless demands on their staff. We know of a managing director who constantly gave his day's output to his secretary at 5 pm, expecting it to be typed that evening. He never asked if she minded or was free to stay on. He got through four secretaries in four months. Any good secretary will work late to get out urgent reports or letters, but it is only considerate to ask if it is convenient.

If you have to share a secretary, don't presume that your work is more important than your colleague's. Discuss the division of time and come to an arrangement. Do not put the secretary in the impossible position of having to take responsibility for sharing out the time between you.

Never criticize a member of staff in front of others. If a client complains about a member of staff, assure them that the matter will be sorted out and deal with it when the client has gone.

Meetings and appointments

Don't call meetings and appointments at unreasonable

times. Your staff have private lives, and regular lunch-time or 5 pm-on-Friday meetings will cause resentment.

Arrive on time for appointments. If you are visiting an office that is new to you, allow time to find it and to find reception. If you arrive early you can always ask the receptionist to delay announcing your arrival. The person you have come to see may have urgent business to finish and ten minutes may be crucial, so don't expect to be seen immediately if you arrive early.

If a visitor arrives on time for an appointment do not keep them waiting. If you are unavoidably detained for more than five minutes let them know with your apologies and a cup of tea or coffee.

THE TELEPHONE

The telephone is the cause of many misunderstandings so it's important to use it with care and to develop a pleasant telephone manner. It's surprising how many people sound irritable or bored on the telephone.

When to use the telephone

Complicated business deals are best sorted out in person, but if business has to be done on the telephone it is wise to confirm the details of a telephone conversation in writing afterwards. Keep the telephone for making arrangements and sorting out straightforward business. If the conversation needs to be lengthy, sort out a mutually suitable time with the person you are 'phoning before you embark, and have all the relevant papers at hand so that you don't have to leave the telephone to search for information.

Answering the telephone

Answer the telephone by giving your name. If you answer someone else's telephone say 'Linda Smith's 'phone' (substituting an appropriate name of course).

The telephonist, receptionist or secretary

If you are responsible for incoming calls you should

answer with a greeting suitable to the time of day and then give the name of the company, department or office. If you have to ask the caller to wait while you locate someone you should regularly inform the caller of the progress made, rather than abandon them to a silent telephone wondering whether they have been cut off or forgotten.

If the caller telephones with an inquiry but is uncertain with whom to speak, a telephonist should help by telling the caller the name and job title of someone appropriate before they put the caller through. On no account should you just connect two parties without explaining to either of them who is calling and who is answering. That just leaves the caller embarrassed and irritated and having to ask who is at the other end of the line.

Taking messages

When answering the telephone note the date and time and ask the caller if there is a message. Write it down if there is and if not, make a note of who called, unless they specifically ask you not to or if they say they will call again later. Always write a message down, never rely on your memory, it will let you down on a busy day.

Answering machines

Telephone answering machines are invaluable to most freelance or self-employed people, but still unnerve people who are unused to them. If a machine answers your call, wait until the tone and then say hallo. Give your name, the day (the person may be away for a few days and need to know when you called) and time you telephoned, and your number. Give a brief reason for the call.

It is discourteous not to respond to messages left on your answering machine.

Disconnections

If a telephone is disconnected in mid-conversation it is up to the person who initiated the call to ring back.

SEXUAL HARASSMENT

Overheard on a train the other day: 'All I did was tap her on the bottom and she accused me of sexual harassment.' The recipient of the tap was right of course; no-one may be that familiar unless invited. It's astonishing that, even today, many people are unaware of what constitutes sexual harassment and have no idea of the distress and fury they cause. It is one form of bad behaviour that should not be tolerated.

Whatever your sex, sexual harassment can be very difficult to deal with, especially if you are being harassed by a superior. Sharp one-liners can work really well, but are best left to those whose wit and confidence see them through tricky situations. Pointing out that such behaviour is mindless and discourteous sometimes works too, as does making sure that you are never alone with the offending party. If it persists the only course of action is to tell someone else, preferably someone in a responsible position, or refer the matter to your union if you belong to one.

THANK YOUS

These are often forgotten. Wherever you work and whatever your job, you should always remember to acknowledge and thank someone who has done a service for you or completed a particularly difficult job. There is an increasing number of freelance and self-employed workers and their services often go unacknowledged. If a freelance worker sends in a piece of work it is extremely bad manners not to acknowledge and respond to it. Thank yous can be made on the telephone if they are for run of the mill work but should be made in writing if they are in appreciation of something exceptional.

SPORTING ETIQUETTE

Sporting etiquette is about consideration for your fellow players and maintaining levels of safe play. 'Being a good sport' does not refer to a person's sporting ability but, more importantly, to the manner in which he plays the game. Some sports have stricter conventions than others. The most difficult area is the body of unwritten rules in all sports which apply only in certain circumstances.

If you are about to begin a new sport, the best way to learn its conventions is to attach yourself to someone who is familiar with them. It is much easier to be put right by a friend than a complete stranger. Never be afraid to ask if you are unsure about something. Experts are usually more than happy to give you the benefit of their advice. It is impossible to cover all sports but in this chapter we shall look at popular sports which have their own code of behaviour.

GOLF

Etiquette on the golf course is central to enjoyment of the game. When playing a round of golf it is important that no set of players holds up the progress of another group. Play should always proceed without delay. Two-ball matches should be invited to pass before three- or four-ball matches as should whole round matches before short round matches. If it looks likely that it will take some minutes to find a lost ball then following players should be allowed to pass.

There should be no movement, talking or other distraction when a player addresses the ball. Players in front should be well out of range before the ball is struck. If in doubt a player should always call 'Fore!' to give warning of his shot. As soon as a hole has been completed the players should leave the putting green.

Looking after the course is also a convention of the game. Holes and footprints in bunkers should always be smoothed over. Similarly, on the green any damage to the turf must be repaired.

A complete novice can be a source of irritation as well as merriment on the golf course. Practice on a driving range should really precede any visit to a golf course, in fairness to the novice as well as the other players.

Some golf clubs frown on certain modes of dress. Trousers tucked inside socks, for example, are not generally approved.

Betting, although officially frowned upon, does take place. The sums involved are nominal and discreet. As in any sport it is bad form to suggest a stake which is outside your opponent's means.

CRICKET

Sportsmanlike behaviour is synonymous with the game of cricket. The code of laws which dictate the game have been adjusted in recent times to suit modern play. These make it quite clear as to what is or is not considered fair play. In all cases the umpire's decision is final. Time-wasting techniques or obstruction carry specific penalties. There are occasions when, although a batsman might be technically out, no-one would appeal for this decision – as in the case of a ball which is stopped before being hit back to the bowler.

The wearing of whites is still a convention of the game as is a handclap following a particularly good shot.

Lords Cricket Ground

The home of the Marylebone Cricket Club (MCC) has some traditions of its own. Whilst on the public terraces anything goes, those with seats in the Pavilion are expected to wear a collar, tie and jacket at all times. Photography is not allowed either in the Pavilion or the long room. During the hours of play the Pavilion is also barred to women.

TENNIS

Although not always observed by the professionals, there are codes of conduct in tennis which are expected at every level. In modern times psychological tactics have crept into the game. Time-wasting and arguing with the umpire are frowned upon, as is any form of play which intimidates your opponent. In a doubles match the idea is to play with your opponent rather than against him. If you miss an easy shot or poach a shot from your partner's quarter, it is courteous to apologize. However, don't take this to excess. A partner who apologizes continually can be a strain on anyones' patience. Non-stop talking or any such distracting behaviour should be avoided. Hoarding balls or sending them back to a neighbouring court while play is in progress will not make you very popular either!

At the end of a match an opponent should be thanked for the game. In a competition match both the umpire and the linesmen should be thanked and their hands shaken.

Wimbledon Fortnight

In the members' enclosure at Wimbledon club members and their guests observe a rule of jackets and ties for the men and smart day dresses for the women.

During matches spectators should only move from their seats when the players are changing ends. Applause is given at the natural breaks in the game – at the end of a game, a set or a match. There is sometimes applause for a particularly fine rally but this can break the flow of play. Distracting behaviour such as eating and drinking in the stands is also discouraged.

SAILING

If you are invited to go sailing it is good manners to make some preparation. Firstly you should tell the skipper if you are likely to be seasick and if you are not able to swim.

Secondly, you should acquire some suitable clothing. This is as much for your own safety and comfort as anything else. Suitable shoes will grip the deck without marking it and waterproof outer wear is essential.

Try to expand your nautical vocabulary before you go. Knowing the difference between port and starboard can make life a lot easier on board.

Cowes Week

Cowes Week on the Isle of Wight is held for one week in August. Entrance to one of the five principal yacht clubs in Cowes is by invitation only. They vary slightly in formality, the Royal Yacht Squadron being the most formal of them all.

Parties are held throughout the week on the larger yachts. Dress is restricted by practical considerations. Long or tight dresses and stiletto heels are not suitable wear on board a yacht.

HORSE RACING

Apart from Royal Ascot and to some extent the Derby and the Oaks, there are no set rules for dress at a racecourse. The object is to 'fit in' rather than to stand out from the crowd. The more glamorous meetings (Ascot, Prix de L'Arc de Triomphe, etc.) attract people not just for the racing but for the social and business connections they may make.

Betting is a serious business and a great deal of thought may go into it before a race. A newcomer to racing should be aware of this and not chatter endlessly about the weather.

Dress, outside Royal Ascot, is usually suited to the occasion rather than high fashion. At Goodwood men may wear the traditional Panama hat, at Newmarket a soft brown hat. Men tend to wear grey worsted suits or tweeds. At winter steeplechase meetings the women will wear coats, boots and headscarves.

Dogs should never be brought to race meetings.

DEATH, FUNERALS & MEMORIAL SERVICES

Today many of the old elaborate rituals of mourning have been discarded. As a result people are sometimes at a loss to know how to cope with their own grief and shock or that of others following the death of a friend or relative. Initially, practical matters keep everybody busy and occupied. The most difficult part often comes later when the funeral is over and everyday life has to be resumed.

When a death has occurred there are several contacts which should be made as soon as possible.

THE FAMILY DOCTOR

The family doctor may issue a death certificate if he has attended the deceased within fourteen days prior to the death or has examined the body immediately after death. The cause of death must be ascertained before a death certificate may be issued. If the cause of death is uncertain the death must be reported to the coroner. This may happen, for example, in the case of sudden death. The death may also be reported to the coroner by a hospital if a patient dies during the course of an operation or by a registrar if he is not satisfied with the information that he has received.

It is the coroner's decision as to whether a post-mortem will take place. An inquest will be held if the death occurred as the result of an accident. Once the medical certificate has been issued or the coroner's authority has been given the death may be registered.

REGISTRATION

A death should be reported within five days and full registration take place within fourteen days. In Scotland the rule is eight days. A death is normally registered by the next of kin – the widow, widower or child of the deceased. Alternatively, it may be the person who found the body or who was present at the death.

When visiting the registrar the following information should be available:

The date and place of death.

The full name of the deceased, including a woman's maiden name.

The usual address of the deceased.

The occupation of the deceased. If married or widowed the name and occupation of the husband.

The date of birth of the surviving partner, if married.

If a child under fifteen, the name and occupation of the father.

THE FUNERAL DIRECTOR

Contact should be made with an undertaker as soon as possible. There is no need to worry about appearing to be in a confused or shocked state. Funeral directors spend their working life with the bereaved and know how to deal tactfully with most situations. The burden of much of the arrangements can be left with them. The funeral director will arrange for the care of the body and help to decide where it will await burial. In some families it is the custom to have the coffin at home for the days preceding the funeral. These days it is more common to have the coffin rest in a chapel or church. The funeral director can also arrange for the coffin to rest at his premises if this is the family's wish.

Sometimes a person makes it clear during their lifetime where they wish to be buried. Whilst there is no legal obligation to do so most people follow these wishes if it is practical to do so.

A common dilemma for many people is the cost of the funeral. It can be a very expensive business and there should be no embarrassment about cutting cost. Many people make it clear during their lifetime that they have no wish for an elaborate funeral. There is no need to purchase the most expensive coffin or to hire half-a-dozen limousines. It is certainly no reflection of your regard for the deceased. However, few people are in the mood for financial discussion at such a time and a good funeral director should make sure that costs do not get out of hand.

CREMATIONS

Arrangements for a cremation are a little more complicated than for a burial. The requirements are:

1 Two cremation certificates signed by the family doctor and another doctor.

2 If the death has been referred to the coroner only the coroner's certificate is required.

3 An application form which must be signed by the next of kin or executor.

4 A third certificate signed by the medical referee at the crematorium. Crematoriums are non-denominational and the form of service and officiating clergyman is chosen by the family.

5 The clergyman.

If the ceremony is to be a religious one the family should contact a member of the clergy of their church as soon as possible. Arrangements for the place of burial may be made as soon as the registrar has issued a certificate for the disposal of the body. It may be that there is a family grave or an arrangement made for a grave space in a churchyard or cemetery. If this is not the case a grave space must be purchased. The date and time of the service must then be decided upon in consultation with the funeral director and the clergyman.

TELLING FAMILY AND FRIENDS

Telling someone that a person close to them has died is never easy. If at all possible this should be done personally. If circumstances prevent this and they must be told quickly, there is often no alternative but to telephone. If the death was unexpected you must allow for the shock that such news will bring. Warn the person that you have some bad news before actually saying what it is. Find out if someone is there with them. If the person is elderly or lives alone it is a good idea to ring someone who lives close by, asking them to visit and give their support.

The recipient of bad news may be distraught or too upset to speak. Allow them time to overcome their initial shock and offer to ring back later. People need a little time to collect their thoughts and to compose themselves before taking in additional information.

Speed in these matters is important as close friends and relatives should be informed directly and not find out by chance. It is courteous to accept offers of help. People sometimes feel the need to show their concern and in the busy days before the funeral it is considerate to allow them to help wherever possible.

ANNOUNCEMENTS

A public announcement of a death may be made through a national or local newspaper. This can also give information regarding funeral arrangements. It may read as follows:

> GREEN on 17 March 19—, peacefully in hospital, Henry George, dearly loved husband of Mary. Funeral service at St Edwards Church, Maidstone on 22 March at 2 pm. Family flowers only.

Newspapers will be able to advise on wording if there is doubt.

ATTENDING A FUNERAL

Dress
Although people generally wear dark colours to funerals there are no longer strict rules of etiquette regarding

dress. It is still traditional, however, for men to wear a black or dark tie and sometimes black armbands if this is the local custom. Invitations are not extended for a funeral. Unless there is an announcement stating that only close family will be attending the funeral, anyone who was known to the deceased is able to attend. Sometimes one person attends to represent a branch of the family or the place of work of the deceased. The latter should make themselves known to the family at some stage of the proceedings.

Flowers and donations

Where it is appropriate to send flowers (i.e., no announcement has been made to the contrary) they are sent to the home or to the undertakers on the morning of the funeral. Sometimes mourners may choose to collect the flowers from the florist and bring them to the churchyard or cemetery. The flowers should be accompanied by a note giving the name of the donor and some message of affection addressed to the deceased – not to the bereaved. Flowers from the immediate family are placed on the coffin.

Sometimes people make it clear before their death that they would prefer donations to be made to a charity of their choice rather than expensive floral tributes. If this is the case, an announcement should be made promptly to prevent orders being placed for flowers.

The funeral service

The chief mourners usually assemble at the house. If the coffin is in the house prayers may be said, led by a member of the family. At the church, the family sit in the front pews on the right of the aisle.

Variations may occur within different denominations. The service may be personalized to some extent. In both the Roman Catholic church and the Church of England the family may consult with the clergy regarding the prayers and hymns contained within the service.

Ashes

Arrangements for the collection of the ashes should be made with the crematorium authorities. It is up to the family to choose the most meaningful way of dealing with these. They may be placed in an urn and kept as a memorial to the dead person. Alternatively they may be scattered over a special place associated with the deceased. If the land is private the owner should be consulted first.

LETTERS OF SYMPATHY

These should be written as soon as possible after receiving news of a death. It is often easier to respond immediately. When one is first moved by grief words come simply and straight from the heart. Don't be afraid to use time-worn phrases if these seem the most appropriate. The letter will be made unique by your own special memories of the deceased. Long after the funeral such letters are read over again as a source of comfort. The bereaved sometimes suffer feelings of guilt – regretting arguments, or feeling that they did not do enough for the deceased during his or her lifetime. Reassure them and remind them of all the positive aspects of their relationship. Lastly, offer support in the days to come. After the activity and bustle of the funeral the bereaved may feel very isolated. The best form of sympathy is to visit the bereaved and to allow them to talk. This is not a morbid occupation but a very positive way to help people through their grief. Etiquette certainly does not demand that the past is not mentioned. Modern manners in these circumstances is as much about being a good listener as finding the right thing to say. It is helpful to indicate that you do not expect a reply to a letter of sympathy.

MEMORIAL SERVICES

A memorial service is usually held for a person who has

been well-known in their profession or in public life. If the funeral has been a private family affair it offers a means for colleagues and associates of the deceased to celebrate the life and mourn the passing of the deceased person.

Unlike the funeral service, the memorial service may be announced well in advance. This is usually done through the national press and may be worded as follows:

A service of Thanksgiving for the life of

Mr Geoffrey Garner

will be held in St Paul's Cathedral on

Wednesday 11 April 19 —

at 11.00am.

This may also be announced as a Memorial Service or, in the case of the Roman Catholic Church, as a Requiem Mass.

Hymns, prayers and bible readings are selected by the family in consultation with the parish priest or vicar. Printed service sheets may be printed with the name of the person for whom the memorial service is held.

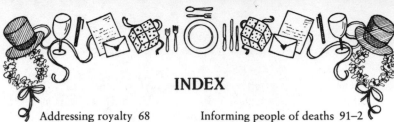

INDEX